THE
EVERYTHING®
GUIDE TO
RAISING A ONE-YEAR-OLD

From personality and behavior to nutrition
and health—a complete handbook

Brian Orr, M.D., and Donna Raskin

Adams Media
Avon, Massachusetts

*To my favorite one-year-olds: Thomas Arnason, Elizabeth
Arnason, and Sam Levinthal—Donna*

• • •

To Patrick, Ailene, and Theresa—Brian

• • •

An Everything® Series Book.
Everything® and everything.com® are registered
trademarks of F+W Publications, Inc.

Published by Adams Media, an F+W Publications Company
57 Littlefield Street, Avon, MA 02322 U.S.A.
www.adamsmedia.com

ISBN 10: 1-59337-727-4
ISBN 13: 978-1-59337-727-4

Printed in the United States of America.

J I H G F E D C B A

Library of Congress Cataloging-in-Publication Data
Orr, Brian G.
The everything guide to raising a one-year-old / Brian Orr and Donna Raskin.
p.   cm. — (An everything series book)
ISBN-13: 978-1-59337-727-4
ISBN-10: 1-59337-727-4
1. Toddlers. 2. Toddlers—Development. 3. Child rearing.
4. Parenting. I. Raskin, Donna. II. Title.
HQ774.5.O743 2007
649'.122—dc22
2006028129

*This book is available at quantity discounts for bulk purchases.
For information, please call 1-800-289-0963.*

Welcome to

THE
EVERYTHING®
PARENT'S GUIDES

A s a parent, you're concerned about your child's growth and development, and you want to ensure that your child grows up happy and healthy. THE EVERYTHING® parenting books are there to guide you along the way, answering questions, dispelling myths, and providing important information from various experts, pediatricians, and other medical professionals and seasoned parents.

The Everything® Guide to Raising a One-Year-Old and *The Everything® Guide to Raising a Two-Year-Old* books are specific guides that take you through your child's various stages of development. This specified series covers crucial topics pertaining to growth and development, emotional development, day-to-day issues, family life, recognizing and rewarding good behavior, avoiding and dealing with bad behavior, learning, nutrition, safety, common illnesses, potty training, and even play time.

The Everything® Guide to Raising a One-Year-Old and *The Everything® Guide to Raising a Two-Year-Old* books are an extension of the successful parenting books in the EVERYTHING® series. These authoritative yet accessible books will help you navigate every year of your child's life, so you can rest easy knowing you have the resources to ensure your child's health, happiness, development, and overall well-being—giving you more time to concentrate on what matters most—your child.

Visit the EVERYTHING® series at *www.everything.com*

The
EVERYTHING®
Guide to Raising a One-Year-Old

Dear Reader,

Although we are both parents and writers, our most significant similarity as the authors of this book is that we enjoy and respect children. We like to play with other people's children on airplanes and sit next to them in restaurants. We like children, no matter what their ages, and find them endlessly fun and interesting.

That said, we have also both had our struggles as parents. We've both been—and struggle not to be—yellers. We have high expectations and have to remind ourselves that children have a right to be children—youthful and learning, rather than always well behaved. At the moment, we have four happy, healthy children between us, but we recognize that as our children grow up, we need to grow and learn with them.

One-year-olds are a million good things, including delightful, bouncy, eager, happy, curious, and fun. This book will answer your questions about health, development, phases, and personality, but we assure you that your love and good humor, as well as your desire to understand your one-year-old, are extraordinary gifts that you are giving your child. You can usually count on them to steer you in the right direction when you're concerned about something.

Brian Orr, M.D.

THE

EVERYTHING
Series

EDITORIAL

Publisher: Gary M. Krebs

Associate Managing Editor: Laura M. Daly

Associate Copy Chief: Brett Palana-Shanahan

Development Editor: Rachel Engelson

Associate Production Editor: Casey Ebert

PRODUCTION

Director of Manufacturing: Susan Beale

Associate Director of Production: Michelle Roy Kelly

Cover Design: Erick DaCosta, Matt LeBlanc

Design and Layout: Heather Barrett,
Brewster Brownville, Colleen Cunningham,
Jennifer Oliveira

Acknowledgments

Thank you, Donna, for the opportunity to work with you. It was my pleasure. You made it easy. Thanks to Bernadette, Patrick, Ailene, and Theresa for putting up with the extra work time I had to spend at the computer.

—Brian

• • •

Thank you to Brian for being the best collaborator I could ever hope to work with, as well as a wonderful doctor to my son. And as always, thank you to Paula Munier, who mothered three children and managed to be a good friend and a great editor, to boot. That's not easy! We also thank Kate Powers, Laura Daly, and Virginia Beck for their editorial skills.

—Donna

Contents

Introduction

YOU PROBABLY HAVE no memory of what your life was like between the ages of twelve and twenty-four months. You probably don't remember being one year old. You don't remember how it felt when you let go of a table and stood on your own, when you tried a new food, or when you noticed that your mother was not actually attached to you. Without your memory to help you, it's often hard to know what exactly a one-year-old needs. When he babbles, is he complimenting you on your cooking? Does he want to get down and play with his blocks? Sometimes it can be frustrating to figure out exactly what this endlessly interesting little person is trying to tell you.

As the parent of a one-year-old, you want very much to know and understand your baby. You love him. You find him fascinating (and cute and fun), and you want to help him and take care of him in the best way possible. While no one can read the mind of a one-year-old, it is possible to benefit from what other parents and experts have learned from the experience of parenting and caring for one. In fact, when you tell someone about an issue you and your child are having, it's always a relief to hear the other person say, "Oh, that happened with us, too! Here's what someone told us to do." For one thing, the solutions often work, but more than that, the exchange of information reminds you that you aren't the first person to experience the problem. Most parents struggle with the same set of issues, such as sleep problems, biting, picky eaters, whining, and crying, which means all these "problems" are actually a normal part of the developmental process—along with adorableness, miraculous moments of learning and growth, and more affection and love than you ever imagined.

Of course, that doesn't mean all one-year-olds are alike. From the shy little boy who stands behind your leg to the little girl who runs down the beach chasing seagulls, every little kid is as unique and interesting as the adults they will become. One of the greatest gifts you can give your child is your own curiosity as well as your acceptance of who he is and how he can best be treated so that he grows up confident and happy. If you wanted a child who loves sports but got a child who loves books, then you need to adjust your expectations, not try to change your child.

This book is meant to do two things. Its first purpose is to reassure you and offer help for those moments when you have a question or are completely baffled. Exactly what are you supposed to do when your daughter won't take off her tiara—*ever*? Is it normal that your son is only happy when the Beatles song "Yellow Submarine" is playing? And why isn't your daughter walking even though she's fifteen months old?

The second purpose of this book is to help you appreciate the process of growing up. As you do, you will realize that you, too, are going through stages and adjustments in your growing-up journey as a parent. You will do and say things that you have always promised yourself you would never do or say. At the same time, there will also be times when other parents look to you for guidance or compliment you on your parenting style or on the behavior of your child.

From crawling to walking, from babbling to making short sentences, from playing alone to sharing a toy, even for just a minute, a lot of changes happen between the first and second year. The toddler whose second birthday you celebrate will be very different from the baby whose party you hosted on her first birthday. Some of these changes will be wonderful, while others may drive you a little crazy; in either case, you will get tired of hearing your parents, your friends, and your baby's caregivers tell you that "It's just a phase." The truth is that at this age, almost everything is just a passing moment and then it's on to the next skill and stage. This is an extraordinary year of development as your baby becomes a toddler. The best part is that you get to come along for the ride.

Chapter 1

Growth and Development

Over the past twelve months, you have seen a lot of changes in your child. From a newborn who couldn't lift his own head, he has grown into a child who can cruise around the living room on his own two feet and communicate with you, responding to your words and maybe pointing or using sounds in response. One day you'll probably glance into your car's rearview mirror and think, "Wow! Look at that! How did that happen?" and then you'll smile and fall in love all over again.

First Steps

Some ten-month-olds stand up and walk solidly across the room. There are fifteen-month-olds who crawl happily from couch to chair to crib, wondering why everyone keeps trying to get them to stand up. Every baby has her own way of progressing from moving around on all fours to standing and walking on two feet. Like so much of parenting, it's best to let your child develop her own process and support her through it. We don't *teach* children to walk as much as simply help them learn how to do it on their own, in whatever way works for them. As long as your child is making progress, don't worry.

Most parents feel reassured by schedules. If a child is walking and talking by her first birthday, then she's "okay." But children develop at their own rate and on their own continuum. Walking and talking are skills that do generally begin around the first birthday and continue to develop throughout childhood. While there is no exact timeline for development, you should notice signs of continuous change and growth.

At the age of one, babies are moving around by any of these means:

- Crawling (moving on hands and knees)
- Creeping (walking with legs straight, hands still on floor)
- Stepping (taking individual steps while holding your hands)
- Cruising (walking while holding onto furniture)
- Walking

Most likely your one-year-old is using a combination of these methods to get around. Some babies take a longer time finding their balance. They can pull themselves up and maintain a standing position while holding onto furniture or your fingers, but they haven't figured out how to stand on their own from a sitting position.

Balance

The word "toddler" comes from the verb "to toddle," which describes an unbalanced way of walking. Toddling refers both to the bolting, lunging steps a baby takes as she starts to sense her balance as well as to the side-to-side movements that one- to three-year-olds make because of their very low center of gravity. If your baby is a cruiser, at some point you'll notice that in moving from the sofa to the coffee table, for instance, she is letting go of one piece of furniture for a second before grabbing the next. This is an important step in learning to negotiate balance.

Stepping and Falling

When babies practice their walking, they often take high, marching steps, lifting their knees and then placing their feet down. Falls are common. Rather than pitching over face forward, babies usually fall right down on their bums, and bumps and bruises are par for the course. Whatever style your baby's walking takes, applaud his attempts and take his falls in stride. Comfort him without overreacting; otherwise, he may begin to believe that falling is scary or dangerous.

Slowing Down

Once she's mobile, your baby will enjoy walking everywhere and may even demand to do so. At this stage, however, she is still too uncoordinated to walk very quickly and too young to orient herself to share your goals—think of all the parents you've seen trying to coax their new walkers into keeping up and taking the "right" direction. Walking along with your toddler is sometimes difficult when you're trying to get something done, like the grocery shopping, in a place that's not necessarily conducive to toddler trial and error, like a crowded grocery store, especially when you're in a rush.

Keep in mind that walking is a huge milestone that takes time and a lot of practice to master. If there are times and places where it is not a good idea for your toddler to walk—like rush hour in the grocery store—try to keep her exposure to these situations as brief as possible. Make a quick trip through the store with her riding safely in the cart, then spend walking time together as soon as possible after getting home. Better yet, make a stop at the park before you hit the store, and let her burn off some walking energy there.

 **Alert!**

> Push toys, such as wagons and carts, help babies balance and move forward. Be sure the wheels are sturdy and that all stairways are blocked so that your child doesn't push the toy—and herself—down a flight of steps. Be sure, too, that there are no wires or cords in your child's way and that all doors are closed securely.

This period of "slow" movement lasts a relatively short time. Most toddlers start running sometime after eighteen months, so stop and smell the roses with your child. Soon you'll be chasing her around and wishing she would slow down.

One Step Up, Two Steps Back

With new freedoms come new fears, and sometimes learning can be scary. Your new walker may suddenly notice that now there is distance separating him from you. As he sees that floor space open up between you and becomes aware of the separation, he may regress in behavior, such as crying more or being clingier than he was before. Understand that all development comes in fits and starts with some bumps along the way. In fact, you, too, may feel a certain sadness knowing that your baby will soon no longer need you to carry him around as much as he used to.

Other Milestones

While walking is definitely the major milestone of motor development, there's lots more that your baby is likely able to do, even if she hasn't started walking. She can pick up smaller objects, such as Cheerios, more easily, and she'll start to try opening doors and turning the tops of jars. She'll also love taking off her clothes, which is much easier for her than putting them on. She'll begin to be able to stack one block on top of the other (a tower of three or four is about as high as it will go this year), and she will be able to turn the pages of a book.

Bending Down

Toward the end of this year, your baby will balance not only when he walks but also when he's standing. You'll notice that he'll begin to bend down and get things off the floor without having to sit, or that he'll twist and look behind himself instead of moving his feet to look around. The best thing about bending down? Your baby can help you pick up toys and will probably enjoy dropping them into a basket or toy chest.

Kicking, Dancing, Jumping, Hopping

Getting comfortable with movement is important at this age, even though actions like kicking, dancing, jumping, and hopping will be awkward. But don't let that stop you from trying things out with your baby! Turn on music and dance for her. Your baby will mimic you. Though she may not move her feet much, she will wiggle her bottom. Roll soft rubber or inflatable balls toward her, and let her try to kick them back to you. Let her try large-wheeled cycles such as low tricycles or Big Wheels so she can get used to moving her legs in circles.

 Question

Is it true that babies who crawl longer and very frequently are smarter?
Too much is attributed to the saying, "You have to crawl before you can walk." Some children walk early and right away, while others crawl even after they can walk. There is no meaning in this behavior, and crawling/walking behavior has no corollary to any other trait.

A one-year-old's attention span ranges from just a few moments to several minutes. It is short because everything around her is new and fascinating. As soon as her eyes rest on a new object, she is interested. Be prepared to accompany your child from toy to toy (or from sofa to floor to bed to kitchen) as she explores the big new world.

Language and Speech Development

By his first birthday, your baby understands a number of words, such as "no," "hello," and some of the names of the people or animals in your family. He is probably starting to make a few sounds with meaning, too, such "hi," which may come out without much of the soft "h" sound but with lots of the hard "i."

When you speak to your baby, look at him so he can see your lips. Speak clearly and somewhat slowly, but don't use baby talk or speak so slowly that the words don't sound natural. Speech is an instinct: The more natural sounds your baby hears, the more likely he is to pick up the meaning and gift of language. Your baby will start to move his mouth around even if he isn't actually making a noise. He's mimicking you (another reason it's good for him to see your lips move) and trying out this new skill.

Babbling

Eventually, your baby will start to use her voice along with her mouth. Her speech will most likely sound like sentences, but only a couple of words will actually be comprehensible, if that. However, you can still figure out what your baby is saying. Most likely, she will be commenting on something in her immediate vicinity, such as a toy that you are playing with, or something she brings to your attention by pointing to it (your earring, for example, or the television). Even if you couldn't pick out any actual words in what she said, you can still respond with something like, "Oh, you like my earring?" Suddenly, you and your child are having a conversation. This is a great milestone. When you respond to her babbles, she learns how wonderful it is to communicate. She will appreciate this validation of her attempts at speech.

Some children are naturally quiet and don't feel compelled to talk as much as some other children might. In a family of talkers, babies are sometimes unable to get a word in to practice their speaking. Older children often talk for younger children. Try to give your child time to speak, or make the room quiet and ask him questions. If you haven't heard the sound of your child's voice consistently by the time he's fourteen or fifteen months old, have his hearing checked.

 **Essential**

Instead of correcting your child's pronunciation, set an example. If he says, "Me want oos," you can say, "You want juice? I want juice, too." This way he knows that he's been heard and, at the same time, he hears both the correct grammar and the correct pronunciation.

Talking to Your Child

Before the age of two, your child will start to string words together in simple sentences, like "Daddy ball?" or "Mommy play?" His sounds will be rough. For example, if a sibling's name is "Samantha," his version might be "Manta." Nevertheless, you should talk to your child properly. He understands many of the words you say, even when your ideas are bigger than the ones he's communicating. You can say, "Yes, Daddy went to get the ball from outside so he can play with you."

Common Vocabulary

At this age, children understand many nouns (people, places, things) and also the concept of possessives (its, mine, yours), which they may even be able to repeat. "My ball!" for example. Your child will ask questions using tone and voice, such as "My ball?" with a tilt of her head, or "No oodles!" with a shake of her head. By the age of two, your child will have a vocabulary of about thirty words that she uses consistently. You can improve her vocabulary by reading to her regularly as well as by using big words even before she can understand them. As she gets older, her vocabulary will reflect the words she's heard.

Social Development

Let's say you meet up with your best friend, whom you haven't seen in a while. You greet each other warmly, and then you spend the next hour talking and laughing together. Your baby might be hiding behind your leg for this greeting, but make no mistake—he is watching you. He is paying attention to cues from you that give him important information about how to behave around other people. Things like your body language, the sound of your voice, and the look on your face tell him that you feel safe and comfortable. He sees that you are happy, that your voice is soft and that you laugh. Even at this early age, he is capable of making associations and beginning to learn that this is the way to behave around friends.

Eventually your child will be able to mimic your behavior in play with other children. At this early stage, however, most children aren't yet sure how to behave with people other than those they see regularly, such as family, day-care providers, and babysitters. Of course, this isn't true of all children; some are gregarious and get right into the thick of things. If your friend has a child, no matter what age, you can encourage your child to play with her. However, keep your expectations age-appropriate. Most children of this age, and even those a couple of years older, are mostly quiet and unable to share. In social situations, your child is likely to look to you for reassurance.

Awareness of Others

Between twelve and twenty-four months, your child is happy to look around and see people in her world, with the key phrase being "her world." She has yet to completely realize that the world isn't hers or that she is a part of a larger universe. Toward twenty-four months, toddlers develop the awareness that the world is also peopled with other, separate individuals; until then, toddlers comprehend other people as extensions of themselves. Twelve-month-olds are capable of empathy (at least briefly). They may be kind and generous, but these actions are not conscious as much as instinctive. In other words, is isn't reasonable to expect this kind of behavior, and you shouldn't expect your child to share or to play nicely with others all the time. Instead, praise her when she behaves the way you would like her to, but remain calm and consistent when she doesn't.

Mirroring

You are your child's role model in many ways, including the words and tone of voice you use, your actions, and the way in which you treat others. While your child may not comment on your behavior, he is likely to mimic it when he engages in pretend play or play with others and in his interactions with you. You'll frequently hear your own words come out of your child's mouth. In fact, experts think that one reason two-year-olds say "no" so often is that they hear it a lot. So try to be on your best behavior in order to set a good example for your child. Watch the words you use—they may come back to haunt you!

 Fact

Empathy and altruism are now thought to be genetic. Although people can be taught to be sensitive to others (and many of us are, even if it doesn't come naturally), it does seem as if some of us are born with a greater capacity for sympathy than others. Optimism and enthusiasm also have a genetic basis.

If a family member or friend doesn't have good manners or behaves badly in front of your child, minimize your child's exposure to her. While this is difficult in terms of family dynamics, the alternative—explaining to your child that some behavior has negative consequences, or that you disapprove of certain actions—is impossible. Once your child has established habits of good behavior, you will be better able to discuss other people's behavior and keep your child from emulating it.

Your Little Helper

Straightening up? Putting the laundry away? Enlist your one-year-old's help. Your child will adore being part of the action and will learn from the job, even if it's something as simple as dropping socks into a basket. After she has helped you complete your task (successfully or not), say thank you. Your child will mimic your use of "please," "thank you," and, of course, the kisses and hugs you give her for a job well done. Starting a helping philosophy early will help your child (and you) later.

Normal Growth Patterns

Sometimes children grow so quickly it seems as if it happens overnight—and amazingly, it actually does. Our bodies grow and rebuild themselves during sleep, which is only one reason that sleep is so important to good health. Aside from this daily growth pattern, there are three main growth periods during childhood. Rapid growth occurs throughout the first year of life; more gradual growth happens during young childhood; and there is another growth spurt during adolescence.

This spurt pattern is also characteristic of other types of growth, such as emotional, social, and intellectual. While you'll notice daily incremental changes in your child's development, you will also experience dramatic changes that seem to occur in a moment. One morning he babbles at the breakfast table; the next morning, he says "Juice!" This growth pattern is completely natural and healthy.

As babies gain mastery over a skill, whether it's walking or playing with a new toy, they often temporarily "lose" a skill they had previously gotten down pat. For example, when they start piling up blocks, they might suddenly stop walking and start crawling again. Or as they start stringing words together, they might start crying when you leave the room, something they hadn't done for the past three months. Don't worry about this.

The learning process is overwhelming for any child, both mentally and physically, especially when you consider that every skill is a new one. In fact, some parents use regression—falling back into old patterns—as a sign that their baby is about to start developing a new skill. Knowing that allows the parent to be more patient and sensitive to the baby's mood changes.

Chapter 2

Emotional Development

One of the most interesting and surprising things about being a parent is that your child is an individual whom you have the privilege of getting to know. Just as you find out more about adult acquaintances the longer you know them, over time you will also learn about your child's personality and preferences. Over the course of your child's second year, you will see him develop not only physically and verbally but emotionally as well.

Temperament and Personality

Temperament can be defined as the prevailing quality of someone's character, the one that the person's close friends would use to describe her—positive and optimistic, for instance, or curious, or wary and fearful. Personality, on the other hand, comprises a wider range of an individual's characteristics, such as her interests, behavior, emotional style, and opinions. Your daughter might have a confident and cheerful temperament, while her love of naps and noisy games would be features of her personality. Your son, on the other hand, might be quiet and somewhat shy by temperament but with a fun-loving personality exhibited in his love of TV time with his father and family mealtimes. In short, you could say that temperament is the mindset we're born with, and personality is the combination of our natural instincts with things we learn.

All of us are born with some natural traits, such as our level of energy, our curiosity in the world around us, and our empathy, while some aspects of our personality are shaped by our environment and experience, such as how warm and affectionate our family is, whether we do well in school, and how much stimulation and growth we are exposed to as children.

Nature Versus Nurture

For the past century and more, parents, educators, and developmental specialists have debated whether nature or nurture is more responsible for determining character. Those in the "nature" camp say a child is born with personality already intact; the proponents of "nurture," on the other hand, believe that the environment surrounding a child is what influences and creates her. In the day-to-day world of a parent, there is a more practical way of considering the issue. It is your job to discover who your child is and to figure out how you can best help him grow up to feel good about himself and do well in the world; how to find a career he can enjoy and be successful in, how to have meaningful relationships, and how to have integrity.

It may seem early to consider these long-ranging issues, but much of what your child learns in his first few years—that he is loved, that he is valued, and that he matters—will have a strong influence on his character as he grows older.

 Fact

> The first three years of life are significant because the more stimulation a child has during this time, the more pathways are forged in his brain. This growth promotes not just intellectual but also emotional and creative development. Likewise, the less stimulation a child receives through interaction, the less likely it is that he will respond well to challenge as he grows up.

Getting to Know Your Toddler

Rather than trying to teach your child a love of classical music or a devotion to football, expose her to all sorts of experiences—all sorts of music, many different sports, as well as arts, the outdoors, and a wide variety of food—and see what she responds to. Pay attention to what seems to make your child comfortable and what overstimulates or bores her. For example, some babies and toddlers love bright lights and noise, while this kind of excitement makes others cry. There is an optimum amount and type of stimulation that fits any given individual's comfort zone. Once parents are tuned in to what their child is capable of and enjoys, they should begin to challenge the child and give her the opportunity to really explore and enjoy those activities.

Boosting Self-Esteem

Self-esteem describes the value you place on yourself as a person and your individual abilities and characteristics. To have high self-esteem means feeling good about yourself and appreciating your intrinsic value, as well as recognizing who you are. The capacity for high self-esteem is largely developed during childhood. When a child is hugged, kissed, loved, and spoken to and taught in a respectful manner, he grows up to believe that he matters in this world, which gives him confidence to build on his inner strength. People with low self-esteem believe they have no value. No matter what they achieve in life, whether it's walking for the first time or winning a baseball game, they still feel like less than a whole person.

To instill a sense of high self-esteem in your child, be curious and accepting of who he is at this stage in his life. Your curiosity about the kind of person he is will help you release expectations that aren't age-appropriate and will, at the same time, make way for acceptance of his one-year-old self. When he lives in a world that accepts who he is at this stage in his life, he will feel encouraged to learn and grow.

While you are teaching your child how to exist in the world, you also want to teach him how to exist within himself—how to speak positively to himself, how to understand himself, and how to take care of himself. High self-esteem and optimism, or a positive outlook, are closely related. Optimistic children are more likely to grow up to be optimistic adults. They do better in school and on the job, are less likely to get depressed, and are healthier than pessimists. Having an optimistic attitude and teaching your child to share it will help him throughout his life.

Keep in mind, though, that helping your child feel good about himself does not mean offering him false praise or half-hearted compliments. Rather than saying, "You are the best little boy in the world," try telling him, "I love the way you helped me put the placemats on the table. Thank you."

Listen to the difference in these two responses to a child's behavior: "You took the baby's toy! You are a bad boy!" and "Johnny, you took the baby's toy away without asking, and that made him cry. Usually you are so nice to him. Next time I'm sure you'll wait until he's finished." When you correct your child, try to use specific examples and to stay away from global pronouncements ("You are a bad boy!").

In terms of promoting your child's self-esteem, there are three good rules to keep in mind. They are useful no matter what situation you're trying to handle, and if you can keep them in mind even when you're frustrated you'll be an effective parent. Here they are:

- Avoid putting negative labels on your child. Never make pronouncements like "You're stupid," or "You are not very good at art." Instead, find a positive way of framing your observations, like "Let's find a better way of doing that" or "Nobody else draws horses the way you do!"

- Correct behavior quickly without berating or shaming your child. Once you have corrected a behavior and the child understands what you expect, do not keep harping on the error.
- Keep praise coming!

Make your negative comment about a specific behavior or action, while leaving room for a positive comment about the child you love and adore.

Validate Feelings

One-year-olds cry fairly often for a lot of different reasons. Tiredness, fear, and sadness are just three of the most obvious reasons. Crying itself can also be scary, especially considering that children don't always know why it is happening.

 Question

My daughter seems unhappy. Is it possible for a baby to be depressed?

Unfortunately, it is, although it's not common. Some people have naturally low energy levels and are somewhat sad. Talk to your physician to make sure she isn't sick in other ways, and then accept her for who she is while still trying to encourage positive, happy feelings as much as you can.

You can help them learn about emotions by identifying their feelings and explaining that crying is a natural reaction. Then offer a diversion. For instance, "Oh, you got scared by the dog. He is big, isn't he? Sometimes we cry when we're scared. But look! Now the dog is gone and the ball is still here." Validating a child's feelings lets her know that her experience is valuable and real and that she can trust her feelings and reactions to her experiences.

Enthusiasm

Another important quality to encourage in your child is enthusiasm, an excitement about whatever it is he's doing. Parents tend to communicate enthusiasm naturally because they are so happy around their children. A wonderful way to encourage enthusiasm in your child is to enlist his excitement about the day ahead.

Describe the events you have planned for the day and what you're looking forward to. This helps reduce stress for your baby because he'll know what's ahead of him; even if he doesn't officially understand everything you say, he'll comprehend your positive attitude. "We're going to the grocery store, the post office, and then stopping at Daddy's office to have lunch. I can't wait to buy some sugar so I can make cookies, and seeing Daddy always makes me happy." Enthusiasm is contagious, after all.

Encouraging Independence

"Me do it!" is a phrase you'll be hearing more and more this year. While it may slow you down to let your child do things on her own, it is important to encourage her independence because it will make her feel confident in her abilities. One day your child will be doing things without you, like going to school or play dates. If she knows you are confident in her abilities, then she will be confident in them, too. You'll see that your child will become upset if she can't do something on her own, so be sure to praise her for trying and for whatever part of the job she did manage to accomplish.

Exposure to New Things

You are in the park with your son and his "best friend." For the first time, they notice the slide with its many steps up and its long ride down. Your son runs toward it and starts to climb. His friend grabs your hand. Your son gets all the way to the top before you can get over to him and make sure it's something he can handle. His friend looks up at the slide doubtfully. Your son begins to cry, terrified, at the top. His friend begins to climb up, not as afraid as he was just a moment ago. Once the pair is together and you're at the bottom, they go down the slide with uncertain looks on their faces. Your son wants to do it again. His friend doesn't.

As the above example illustrates, everyone approaches new experiences differently. What's more, different people place different values on those experiences. Your child may be shy and hesitant about trying new things and may prefer to concentrate on a few favorite activities, or he may want to try everything once. Regardless of your child's personal style, the important thing is for you to offer new experiences in a safe and confident manner. Eventually your shy child will be ready to add a new activity to his routine, and at some point the "try anything once" child will find something that he wants to do again and again.

The way we approach new things does not predict the outcome of our experience. Try to understand and accept your child's behavior toward new things without judgment. Then talk and support him through all the new things he's going to encounter as a child. This is the best way of ensuring that your child is receptive to being exposed to new experiences.

The Bold Child

If your one-year-old runs fearlessly up to dogs, enters rooms without hesitation, and immediately says "Hi!" to children and adults, you know that it may not be necessary to encourage her to try new things. Instead, you might need to teach her respectful boundaries, such as not touching strangers and not grabbing toys from other children. A bold child can overwhelm others, so it's important to help your child not be bossy or controlling, which is just as off-putting to others as extreme shyness. Don't discourage confidence, but monitor her behavior so that other parents and children enjoy having her around.

 Alert!

Most parents talk about their children in front of them. For example, they might say things like "He's shy" or "He just learned how to put on socks!" This is a great thing to do as long as comments are positive, but it's not great to voice negative opinions publicly. Remember, your children understand you before they can repeat what you say.

The Shy Child

Before venturing out into a new situation, most children will stand behind their mommy's legs, hold their daddy's hand, and look around the room (sometimes for a long while). This isn't shyness as much as a natural instinct—after all, figuring out a situation before jumping into it is a survival strategy. Don't force your child to behave in a way that is unnatural to him. Let him look around, stand close to you, and get used to the situation you are in. Chances are that, in a few minutes, he will see something or someone that intrigues him and he will move toward it. You can gently encourage him to explore, so that he knows you believe he is safe.

Keep in mind that shyness is a personality trait. Many shy adults recognize the quality in their children. If you have a shy child, don't humiliate him by dismissing this trait and forcing him to act in a way that is uncomfortable and unnatural for him. Shyness is not a character flaw or a weakness; it is simply a characteristic that can be handled so that it won't inhibit friendships or success in school.

Prepare your child for the day by explaining what he's going to encounter. Let him take his time getting used to a new place. Once you're back in the car or at home, praise him for the good job he did. This will help him feel more confident about taking on the next new experience.

Separation Anxiety

Time doesn't mean much to a small child. One-year-olds obviously can't read clocks, and they won't really start to understand measures of time—like "a day" or "two hours"—until they are older. When you leave, your child has no way of knowing that you will be back after awhile; she may very well believe you are gone for good. Learning that people come and go from hour to hour and from day to day is one of the most difficult lessons of childhood.

"Separation anxiety" is a term that describes how truly upset and uncomfortable children become when their parents or other loved ones leave. Crying and tantrums are not uncommon and should not be dismissed or mocked. Instead, you need to acknowledge how your child is feeling and explain that you will be back.

Do not make your leaving long and drawn out, as this will increase your child's worry and will also begin to make her sense that you, too, are upset about leaving. While of course you don't want her to think you don't care, you also want her to see that you are confident and feel safe and secure. Give her a kiss and a hug, tell her "Goodbye, I love you, and I'll see you later," and then leave quickly, even if you feel like your heart is breaking—don't worry, you'll be back soon!

 Fact

In the first few weeks of a new care-giving routine, some children do cry for an extended period. Once they get used to the new routine, however, it is very rare for a child to cry for hours. Most children cry for half an hour at most and then settle in.

Most children at this age do go through extended periods of separation anxiety. They can cry for hours, which can be heartbreaking for a parent or caregiver. But this type of distress has no impact in terms of long-term trauma or even on the child's ability to separate later in life.

Leaving Your Child with a Caregiver

If you have to leave your child regularly, for instance, to go to work every day, the best way to help your child deal with the separation is to work into it slowly. Begin by introducing your child to her new caregiver and incorporating this person into your daily routine. In the days and weeks before you return to work, have the caregiver spend time with you and your child, doing the ordinary things you usually do together. This way, your child will associate the new person with you and will not be as anxious when you are gone and the two of them are alone together. If you will be taking your child to a day-care center, be sure you select one that allows you to make multiple preparatory visits with your child. With you at her side, she will be more secure and confident about the new place, the new adults, and especially all the new children. She will also be better equipped to handle separation from you when the time comes for you to leave her there for the day.

The same principle applies when you are preparing to leave your child for shorter periods. At some point, for instance, you will probably want to go out in the evening and leave your child at home. Begin by talking to your child the night before so she has time to assimilate the idea. Introduce her to her babysitter, preferably ahead of time. Let her see you explain her routine to the babysitter, and make sure this person knows what makes your child comfortable. Reassure your child that you will be there when she wakes up, just like always.

Talking Through Fear

Too often parents assume that intellectual explanations won't soothe their young children's fears. Although your child is very young, with an immature grasp of language and communication, talking to him about his fears is still the best way of helping him handle them. Identify the things that frighten him, and then explain them as simply as you can with a demonstration if possible. Lightning is caused by electricity in the sky (turn a lamp on and off to show the connection); thunder is just a clap of air (you can make thunder noises with your mouth and hands); dogs bark to say hello; and the dark happens when the earth turns away from the sun and the moon comes out (show him the moon).

 Essential

Many children exhibit a fear of strangers, and it's sometimes difficult to determine if their anxiety is the result of fear that you are leaving, fear of the person they are being left with, or a combination of both. Do not force your child to be friendly to someone he isn't yet ready to trust. He needs to learn to trust his instincts.

While this approach may not cure your child of his fears, it will help him understand that the things he is afraid of are not mysterious—they are natural occurrences that you are familiar with and capable of explaining. Everything is new and unexpected to a child; by talking, you are demonstrating that these things that are strange and frightening to him are normal parts of life. This takes away the unexpected element of the scary moment. Don't react too strongly to a child's fears. Once again, the calmer you are, the calmer he'll be.

Children are commonly afraid of the dark and of lightning and thunder, animals, and loud noises. That's one reason these things feature so prominently in so many stories and movies. Bring your child to the library and look for age-appropriate books about these topics. Reading such a story in a nonimmediate moment (that is, when the dog isn't barking or the thunder isn't clapping) is another way to soothe his worries.

Sharing and Taking Turns

At one year of age, children have not yet developed the social or emotional maturity to play together, whether in pairs or in bigger groups. For one-year-olds, the term "playing together" means little more than sitting near each other. Each child is absorbed in her own individual activity. The children do not share games, toys, or imaginary play; the most they can be expected to do is perhaps take notice of each other's toys and maybe try to take what they find interesting for themselves. While they enjoy being in groups for physical fun like singing or dancing, they don't actually share the experience with their friends by singing or dancing with each other. Instead, one-year-olds view the experience as their own—other children are just extensions of the moment.

If you want to get your child used to sharing, you're going to have to direct the play. Say that you have a ball that your child and her friend both want to play with. You might try sitting on the floor with them and rolling the ball first to one and then to the other. Again, the children will be playing near each other and with the same toy, but they are not really playing together. Do not expect them to take turns. That's a lot for them to grasp at this age.

Typical Behavior

When playing in groups or with another child, your child will enjoy rolling balls, playing with large puzzles, dancing, singing songs (especially ones with clapping and hand movements), finger painting, and playing outside. Most children also love dress-up at this age, not so much for the possibility of pretend play as for the challenge of getting in and out of the clothes and seeing how different they look in the mirror. In fact, it's a great idea to have a large mirror around, as young children love to look at themselves. When it comes to toys, it's best if each child has his own to avoid the disputes that are so common at this age.

 Fact

It's largely a waste of time to ask a child "Why did you do that?" Simply set an example. "John didn't know you were still playing with that block, James. You can have it back." Then give John another toy. Fairness is important, as chances are James will take a toy from John in a moment.

Supervising Play

Because it is unrealistic to expect a one-year-old to share with others or to engage in self-directed play, you will have to encourage and take part in playing with your child and her friends. They will want you to play with them, anyway, and will bring blocks and other toys over to you (even if you're busy). It's helpful, then, to realize that your presence is necessary. They are watching you closely to see how you play, share, take turns, and enjoy yourself.

Your job, if you are playing with your child and any of her friends, is to offer them all the same instruction, praise, guidance, and correction. Do not be tougher on your child because you want her to make you proud and do not, on the flip side, play favorites with your child. While this is often difficult for a parent, your child wants to see and hear fairness more than she wants favoritism. This is what she will encounter out in the world, and by setting the example of kindness and fairness you will help her be a good friend when she is ready to be one.

Teaching Manners

At this age, your child may not be able to say "Please" and "Thank you," but it's still important for you to model good behavior for him. If you speak to him as politely as you would to other children and adults, those words will become part of his speech habits. Ask nicely and with respect when you want your child to give you a toy or to help clean up, and then thank him when he does as requested. This will show him how you expect him to behave toward others.

You might also want to consider how you would like your child to address other adults. Will it be Ms. Smith or Ms. Alice? Do you want him to say "Yes, ma'am" and "No, sir"? Or do you live in a more casual world where first names are fine for grownups? Consider, too, asking the preference of the adults involved.

Hello, Goodbye, Please, and Thank You

Babies start to wave bye-bye between eight and twelve months, but at this point they are more mimicking your motions than using the wave as a means of communication. Nevertheless, most parents encourage their children to say "Hello," "Goodbye," and other niceties. However, don't expect it of your one-year-old, and don't be surprised if he doesn't do as you ask right away. You can also try saying it for him, such as, "Peter had a lovely time here today, Paula, thank you so much for the cookies." Eventually, he'll make eye contact with the person and feel more comfortable using the words himself.

"Modeling" is the word development experts use to describe what parents and caregivers do to demonstrate how they would like children to behave. A lot of this behavior is unconscious—how many of us think about the way we speak from moment to moment? But when a one-year-old is watching you, you need to model the kind of behavior you want to see in him later on.

Waiting Is the Impossible Part

Now. Now is really the only time that exists for a one-year-old. Waiting and time are alien concepts. One-year-olds will tug on you, put things in your hand, and try to get your attention when you're already busy, so you need to stay patient and have realistic expectations. The best thing you can do is to explain that you are busy, acknowledge what they are trying to show you (this alone might be enough to stop the interruption), and tell them you will be with them soon. They won't really understand that, but they'll get used to it. Eventually you will be able to say, "You need to wait."

In order to get your child used to waiting and being patient, you must do two things. First, after your child has successfully managed to be even a little bit patient, be sure to ask her about what she wants to show you or tell you. She needs to know that you aren't ignoring her. Second, thank her for waiting (even if she really didn't wait that long).

Chapter 3

Day-to-Day Issues

All the advice in the world about intellectual development and personality issues is nothing compared to one moment of real life in the life of your one-year-old. This chapter addresses common, every-day issues such as tooth-brushing, going to the store, blankies, baths, getting dressed, and the other rou-tines of daily life. The more fun you make these small moments, and the more you are able to see them as times to connect with your child, the more you will be thinking like your one-year-old.

Bathing

At one, your child is sitting up in a bathtub and probably loves being in the water. If she doesn't like it, her unhappiness is usually due to some factor you can figure out and change. Is it water temperature? Boredom with the toys? Tiredness? Whatever it is, there are ways to make baths more entertaining for your child and even, believe it or not, an effective ritual for cleaning.

 Question

What if my child is afraid of water?
Is he afraid he's going to go down the drain? Of slipping? Of the running water? You can try getting in the tub with him or have him play in the tub without water. You might also let him watch you or another adult or child take a bath so that he sees how the process goes.

Because they are so mobile and curious, one-year-olds get dirty pretty quickly, which means that baths are a regular necessity. You don't have to give a bath every single day, but they should be regular—at least every other day to every two days. Regular baths not only make a child more comfortable, but they cut down on germs and thus illnesses.

It is important for everyone in the family to wash their hands regularly and often, as clean hands prevent bacteria from spreading from person to person. In fact, antibacterial wipes are one of the best products for any family to keep around—in the car, the living room, the kitchen, the bathroom, and in the diaper bag—because they allow you to quickly and easily wipe away germs.

Too many baths can lead to dry skin, so if you bathe your child frequently be sure to keep bath time as brief as possible. If your baby's skin is dry, stay away from water that is too warm. Putting nonallergenic lotion on immediately after bathing will "lock in" the moisture from the bath. Nonallergenic lotions are the safest for young skin because other products, such as those with petroleum and fragrances, can cause reactions.

All-natural products, which typically contain essential oils and no chemicals, are often the safest for sensitive skin. If you notice small bumps on your child's skin, it's possible she has an allergy to a soap or lotion, so try something else. Just because a product says it's intended for babies doesn't mean that it's best for their skin. Read the ingredient list and look for natural oils and ingredients rather than a long list of chemicals.

Making Baths Fun

To a one-year-old, baths aren't about cleanliness but about having their bodies in a new place surrounded by a new and unusual element that's not solid, that changes temperature, and that moves through the child's fingers and changes shape. Before you start cleaning your baby, play with him in the water and help him get to know it. Let the water drip from your fingers, splash a little, and talk about the way it looks and feels. Your enthusiasm about baths will encourage your child to be excited about bath time.

Another way to make bath time fun is to make a bubble bath. Children love bubble baths, but the bath solution is often made from very harsh detergents, such as sodium laureth sulfate, a common ingredient in detergents, soaps, and shampoos. These can irritate skin, especially the sensitive genital area of little girls.

Look for bubble bath that is made of natural ingredients. Natural soaps and bubble baths use vegetable-derived ingredients, so you'll recognize the words in the ingredient list. These may froth a little less, but they are safer for your child and less likely to cause skin irritation. You can find these bubble baths, soaps, and shampoos in the natural food section of your grocery store. Be sure to completely rinse bubble bath off to avoid irritation.

 Alert!

Don't let your child play with the faucet. If he accidentally turns on the water, he could get burned. Make sure your water heater is set at 120 degrees or lower. At the same time, make sure the water doesn't get cold while your baby is in the tub. If it does, add hot water carefully and away from your child.

Be sure to have a couple of bath toys such as a cup, a ball (some of them are made to be soaked and then squeezed dry), and, of course, some rubber duckies. For safety's sake, keep the water level low (about four inches), the temperature warm but not hot, and keep your child sitting, rather than standing, in the tub. If a child slips in the bath, he could drown—even in shallow water—so never leave a child alone in the tub.

How to Clean a Child

Cover your baby's eyes and pour water over her head. Pour a little bit of a gentle baby shampoo into your palm. Rub your hands together, then gently massage it into your child's hair. Use your fingertips to massage her scalp—rather than her hair. The scalp is really what you want to wash, since her hair gets washed when the shampoo is rinsed out. Covering her eyes again, pour water over her head to rinse off the shampoo.

Now, use baby soap on a sponge or washcloth to wash your baby, being sure to keep the soap away from the eyes, nose, and mouth. Be gentle and then rinse her off with a clean washcloth.

Cut or file your baby's finger and toenails with a baby nail clipper or a fine emery board, but don't try to clean inside her ears. Using a cotton swab can potentially lead to infection or earaches.

Tooth-Brushing

Children need their teeth brushed twice a day, once after breakfast and once before bedtime. Use a soft-bristled brush as well as toothpaste with fluoride. You only need a very small amount of toothpaste; it's really the brushing that does the job, not the paste.

Some children don't mind getting their teeth brushed, some hate it, and some want to do it themselves. Whatever the situation, most children are happy to do some of the job themselves. If your child wants to brush his own teeth, let him, but then do another brushing for him to make sure his teeth have been brushed thoroughly enough. Tell him that the two of you are taking turns. Once he has had his turn, you can make sure his teeth are brushed properly.

Fair's fair. If necessary, you may need to let your child brush your teeth. Show him that you enjoy the process and that you trust him to do a good job. When he's finished, show off your nice clean pearly whites.

Brushing is very important for young children. Even though they will lose their baby teeth, cavities are painful and can cause problems in adult teeth that haven't yet come in. Cavities are also likely for children who inherit the tendency toward unhealthy teeth. If you notice holes in your child's teeth or if your child complains about pain in his mouth, take him to a dentist to have his teeth checked.

 Essential

If your child chips or hurts a tooth, bring her to the dentist immediately. Try to bring the tooth with you in a cup of milk, because milk has nutrients the tooth's root cells need to stay healthy. A dentist can also make sure there is no damage that might cause problems with your child's adult teeth.

The number-one thing you can do to prevent cavities is to brush your child's teeth carefully after meals and before he goes to bed. What really hurts teeth is leaving foods, including milk or juice, in the mouth for long periods of time (such as overnight). It used to be thought that cavity-prone teeth and bleeding gums were unhealthy in and of themselves; now, however, dentists and researchers believe that some people's mouths don't fight bacteria as effectively as they should, which is what leads to mouth problems, including cavities. Brushing and rinsing are important.

Getting Dressed

Some children happily put on any clothes you set out for them, getting dressed in two minutes flat and never thinking about how they look. Then there are children who notice colors and textures and struggle to dress themselves, even when they are still too young to manage the buttons and zippers on their own.

When your child turns one year old, you will still be dressing her. As the year progresses, however, your child will begin to be able to slide a dress over her head, pull pants or leggings on (tights will be tough for years!), and get her arms into a shirt. You may have to help her with buttons and zippers, but she'll want to try them herself. The more you can let her do on her own, the better she'll feel about herself.

Choosing Clothes

Children tend to love fun clothes—with large pictures of the things that they like, such as princesses or trucks or favorite TV characters. If your child has a favorite character or motif, you can buy clothes featuring that design with the knowledge that he will be happy when he is dressed. Still, you should think comfort first and *then* appearance when choosing clothes for your child. If he loves to run and jump, don't dress him in such a way that his clothing impedes his movements.

If he loves to get messy, be sure he has clothes that he can get dirty without making you too worried about cleaning them. Keep in mind when choosing clothes that some children are very sensitive to itchy materials, preferring cotton rather than wool and acrylics. Likewise, sensitivity can manifest itself in a dislike of turtlenecks, long sleeves, and heavy clothes. Be sure you listen to your child's preferences in terms of comfort.

 Alert!

While most parents put hats on their children to keep them warm in winter, hats are also important in summer to protect from sunburn. Wide-brimmed hats, especially those with brims in back to protect the neck, are especially helpful.

Make sure the clothes you get are easy to get on and off for quick diaper changes. If your child gets dirty fast, consider using layers—such as a short-sleeved T-shirt over a long-sleeved shirt, so that when the first shirt gets dirty, you can just take it off and your child will still be dressed in something clean.

Even if you aren't always carrying a diaper bag these days, have an extra change of clothes in the car or nearby when you're going out for the day. It's always best to be prepared!

Reducing Struggle

Most of the struggle involved with parents and children stems from unrealistic expectations and time issues. Your child needs time to get dressed in the morning. She isn't aware of the clock, meetings, work, or a schedule. She is actually exhibiting maturity when she concentrates on buttoning a shirt or trying to put on her shoes all by herself. While it's difficult not to rush children, it's much more effective to give them the time they need—or at least some time—to try to get themselves dressed and ready for the day.

If you believe your child is a dilly-dallier, the first thing to do is eliminate distractions. Turn off the television, sit down on the floor with her clothes, and hand her each item, one at a time, helping her as needed. This should take about ten minutes. That may seem like a long time, but it's ten minutes well spent compared to any length of time spent yelling and pleading and rushing.

Shoes

These days, shoes are all about Velcro. In fact, many children don't have to struggle with laces until their fingers are quite able to manipulate strings easily. If Velcro looks too informal on some occasions, look for large buckles rather than laces. Your child should always wear shoes in public places, but feel free to keep him barefoot or in socks when he is in your house. Socks with textured bottoms can give your baby some security on smooth or slick floors without forcing his foot into an uncomfortable position.

Another easy option is to have your child wear boots like Wellingtons. Children love boots, and many will wear them no matter what time of year or weather. Rain boots are easy to pull on and slip off and allow kids to get messy in mud, water, and dirt. These might be their favorite shoes even on dry days. Clogs and other slip-ons are also popular. Make sure your child's shoes fit properly and aren't worn out. You will probably need to replace them every six months at least.

 Question

Why does my child always want to be naked?
It feels good! At this age, there shouldn't be any embarrassment on your part or your child's. While his body and feet should be covered in any public place, your child should be able to run through your house and back yard naked. For cleanliness and health, be sure he has a diaper on.

Thumb-Sucking

Some babies start sucking their thumbs or fingers as newborns, while others never have the desire to put their fingers in their mouths. Don't worry about it at this age. Even if your child continues for years to suck her thumb, she will eventually only do it when she sleeps or is very tired.

If you are concerned that your child's thumb-sucking is getting in the way of her learning to speak or using her hands, try not to take her hand out of her mouth or make her conscious of what she's doing. Instead, say something like, "I can't understand you with your thumb in your mouth," which gives her the choice to remove his thumb.

Keep in mind that pacifiers are different from thumbs. The World Health Organization recommends against pacifier use because it requires the parent to supply something to the child rather than letting the child independently develop the habit of soothing herself. While sucking is a natural reflex, a pacifier is not natural. The pacifier may signal to a one-year-old that crying is unacceptable, even though crying is one of a one-year-old's few means of communication. Some people also believe that thumb-sucking is an easier habit to break than pacifier use. At this age, you might want to consider weaning your child from the use of a pacifier. If your child uses a pacifier a lot, try to decrease the amount of time it is available to her. Most daycare centers and schools will discourage the use of a pacifier.

One unintended consequence of thumb-sucking is irritation of the skin, caused by the constant moisture and the friction of teeth and tongue. You may need to put an adhesive bandage on your one-year-old's thumb if the irritation gets red and painful. If you use lotion to soothe your one-year-old's skin, be sure it is safe for him to ingest and contains no petroleum byproducts or other toxic chemicals. If the skin gets too raw, talk to your doctor about creams or ointments that are safe to use (even if they end up in your child's mouth).

The taste of the lotion or the presence of a bandage will discourage thumb-sucking to an extent (although your child may be one of the rare children who will suck either thumb, not just one). You might need to alternate these solutions with time for her to suck her thumb, keeping in mind that your child is sucking her thumb as a way of reassuring and soothing herself. Try not to make the irritation a source of conflict. The calmer you are about the thumb-sucking, the easier it will be for your child to give it up when she needs to.

Fears

Your child comes running over to you and stands behind your legs. Or he suddenly starts to cry and you can't figure out what happened. Once your baby starts interacting more with the world, he may go through fearful periods. Previously, your baby cried if he was hungry, tired, or missed you. Now, however, he is far more aware of the outside world, and while it is often thrilling, it is sometimes overwhelming as well.

It is never okay to dismiss a child's fears or tease him about them. If feelings aren't acknowledged, validated, and resolved, then they show up in other ways later on. Always take the time to help your child with his feelings. It is only in this way that he'll feel happy and whole inside. Try following this routine. First, acknowledge that you understand your child's feelings: "I see that you are afraid." Next, share your feelings: "I don't see anything to be afraid of." Finally, reassure him that everything will be all right: "But I want to keep you safe."

As a grownup, you can put everything you see and hear into context—you know what your world is supposed to look and sound like. Children are still meeting the world, and it's up to you to let them know they are safe.

The Dark

Fortunately for children, most adults understand why the dark is scary: When you can't see what's out there, your imagination tends to fill in the blanks. Luckily, it's easy to reassure your child that there is nothing in the dark that isn't there in the light. One of the most effective and fun ways to do this is to go on a search for monsters (or whatever your child is afraid of) using a flashlight. Open boxes and closet doors, look under beds, and search behind toys. Showing your child that she is safe, rather than just telling her, will help her see the truth. It will also help her feel more capable of dealing with her fear because she will be involved in reassuring herself.

 Fact

One of the best ways to help deal with a child's fear of monsters is to read about them. Three great books for young children about monsters are *Go Away, Big Green Monster,* by Ed Emberley; *Leonardo the Terrible Monster,* by Mo Willems; and *My Monster Momma Loves Me So,* by Laura Leuck.

If your child is still afraid, you can offer her a stuffed animal or toy to hold onto, but do all you can to have her sleep in her room. Do not bring her into your room because she's afraid. If you do this, she may feel that you, too, believe there is something to be afraid of. While some parents sleep with their children, it's important to make sure this doesn't become a habit mired in your child's feelings of fear. In other words, sleeping together needs to be separate from fears or worries. If you can communicate to your child that she is safe in the house no matter where you are, then she will feel more secure in general. Your confidence ends her fear.

Being Alone

One-year-olds are in the process of slowly developing an awareness that their bodies and the needs of their bodies are separate from you, as well as from others. Previously, their food supply and the comfort you gave them was almost immediately available. Now, as your child develops more independence, he'll suddenly find himself across the room from you, his source of all things good. Just as you're enjoying watching him display his confidence in his ability to walk away from you, you'll suddenly see him look up in a panic as he realizes you are farther away than usual. The combination of short-term memory, newfound independence, and fear of losing you can create interesting moments of confidence and worry in a one-year-old. He'll run a few feet from you, play, then look up and start to cry. And all of this will happen in a minute. It's confusing for him and can be confusing for you.

 Essential

Your child may not know why he's afraid, but you shouldn't be afraid of taking a guess. Saying, "Are you afraid because you didn't know where I was?" will not put ideas in his head. Quite the opposite is true; he'll feel calmer because he knows you understand and are helping him understand his feelings for himself.

"It's okay. I'm right here," you'll say to your suddenly hysterical baby, which will reassure him because he can see you and come over to you. But this same fear may repeat itself a few hours later when you put him to bed and he starts to panic because he sees you walking away. This fear is different than a fear of the dark, although he may not be able to communicate that. As you do to ease other fears, such as a fear of the dark, you might need to walk your child through the process of separation. In other words, show him where you are and explain that you don't leave or go away when he's asleep. You might even reassure him that you check on him when he's sleeping. Explain that you sleep at night, too, but that you can hear him and that you feel safe.

Remember that these experiences feel new to your child. He may have been sleeping soundly for the past year without a worry, but now he's suddenly conscious of what's happening, and it is this awareness that causes his fear. While it may feel surprising that he's suddenly afraid, remind yourself that it is a sign of his growing understanding of his independence.

Animals

In the case of animals, a little fear is a mighty good thing. Teaching your child to be cautious around animals and to treat them with a healthy level of respect can help keep her safe from bites. Show your child how to introduce herself to a dog or cat by displaying her hand, palm up, and not looking into the animal's eyes directly.

If a dog runs over to your child, be sure to pick her up; you don't know how the dog behaves around small children. Explain to your child that you aren't afraid of dogs, but that you want to be careful since you don't know this one. Then, once you've determined that the dog is child-friendly (by asking the owner, not by your own instinct), you can use this as another opportunity to show your child how to be friends with an animal. Cats are also capable of scratching a child who approaches it too quickly, so walk over to a kitty and show your child how you approach one—quietly and also with your hand out. It is also important to teach young children how to pet animals nicely. You can calmly pet a dog or cat together so that you can show your child how to be gentle.

First Haircuts

To a mom, haircuts are a fabulous luxury. A relaxing hour during which someone actually washes your hair for you and then makes you feel beautiful—what could be better? But to a small child, a haircut only means one thing: a pair of scissors coming at her. Somehow even one-year-olds know that can't be good. At some point in the next twelve months, you'll probably have to cut your child's hair. If she's calm about it, great, but if not you'll need to do some prep work.

The first and best thing you can do is to take your child and a friend with you when you get a haircut yourself. Or go with a friend who is getting her hair cut. This way, your child will see that there's nothing frightening to you about a haircut. You can also take her to a salon that specializes in cutting children's hair. These salons usually have fun seats shaped like airplanes or thrones, and the stylists have experience helping children feel comfortable. Plus, they know how to cut their hair!

If your child gets really frightened at the salon, you might try cutting a small piece of your hair at home on your own. This way, she'll see that it doesn't hurt and you can show her the hair after you've cut it. Some one-year-olds don't need to worry about haircuts because not all children have lots of hair at this age. In fact, you may be concerned that your child—boy or girl—will never get a full head of hair. Don't worry—it will happen! In the meantime, you may want to dress your daughter up by putting a barrette or ribbon in her hair. If so, do this only for short periods of time, and make sure it's not too tight. Her hair is delicate at this age, and pulling it too much can make it thinner. Also, babies tend to pull barrettes out, which defeats the barrette's purpose and can break their hair.

Day Care

Day care is one of the most emotionally and politically charged issues in parenting. While many people feel that a parent should stay home with the children, economics, personal preference, and family situations often mean that mother and father both work during the day. Most working parents take their children to day care for part or all of the day.

Research has shown that day care, in and of itself, is not harmful to children. Under certain conditions, it can often be helpful. Learning, being around other children, and socializing with adults other than their parents can improve intellectual and social skills. The Abecedarian Project (online at *www.fpg.unc.edu*), for instance, studied the effects of highly structured day care on children of very-low-income families; the study found that high-quality day care indeed enhanced those children's grasp of the ABCs and mathematical skills and gave them better success in adulthood as well.

What to Look For

The key word when it comes to day care is *quality*. Looking for a good day care facility is not the same as looking for a babysitter or a school. A young child needs safety, love, affection, support, and stimulation. In this case, safety means that there are enough teachers that no children are unsupervised and that the teachers pay close attention to all the children.

A safe day care facility must also be clean. This is important to help fight infections and contagious illnesses. It's very difficult to keep both children and a room full of them and their things clean, but you should get the impression that the center is doing all it can.

Make sure, too, that the facility you choose doesn't sit the children down in front of the television every day. There are a number of reasons that television and movies are a problem at day care. First, a one-year-old doesn't benefit the way an older child might from watching even educational children's programming. Second, when one-year-old children are in front of a television screen, no one is interacting with them, which leaves them feeling bored and even scared because in essence they are alone. Third, when young children are in front of the television, especially in a group, they can get rowdy and out of control because the television doesn't really hold their interest enough; at the same time, the noise and constantly changing picture is agitating to them. Finally, you're not paying the television to babysit your child.

Next, ask yourself whether the caregivers seem genuinely loving, kind, and concerned about the children. At this age, intellectual rigor and intensity is less important than warm and friendly faces, as well as nurturing and support.

Different Types of Facilities

Some day care centers are home-based, while others are independently owned. Still others are franchises of large corporations. Each of these types of centers has its pros and cons, although studies have shown that home-based day care—where one or two adults care for a small number of children, some of which are often their own—is the least likely to help a child develop social and learning skills.

If you are worried about the potentially negative consequences of day care, discuss these with your caregiver and do research about how to minimize them. The most commonly reported negative impact of day care comes from the number of hours a child spends there and a rise in aggressive tendencies. It seems as if children who spend more than thirty-nine hours a week in day care behave more aggressively. It is unclear, based on the research, if this is truly a consequence of day-care quality or a reflection of other issues, such as a lack of time with parents. It does seem safe to say that high-quality day care is a positive influence, whereas poor-quality day care that takes precedence over time spent with the family does not help a child develop. And the price of day care isn't always a sign of quality. In fact, Head Start programs, which are often subsidized, have been shown to benefit children, especially those from low-income families.

Visit a day care center with your child and try to spend a few hours there, watching the routine, and the way the children are cared for. Do the children who are there seem happy, stimulated, and interested in their surroundings? Do the teachers follow a routine that seems logical? Are there comfortable areas for playing and sleeping? The following list of questions includes day-to-day information you'll need, as well as some points of discussion for you and the day care director and teacher. You can photocopy the list and bring it with you as you visit facilities.

► Questions to Ask a Day Care Provider

What is your policy about late arrivals and pickups?

....

....

How are meals handled?

....

....

How is diapering handled?

....

....

What are the naptimes? How are children put to sleep?

....

....

How many children are in a class?

....

....

What is the policy about illness?

....

....

How do you teach children good behavior?

....

....

How do you handle children who haven't learned how to share?

....

....

What are your expectations of children at this age?

....

....

What is the day's schedule?

....

....

What are the day's activities?

....

....

How do you communicate with parents?

....

....

What do you feel you offer to the children?

....

....

What do you expect from parents?

....

....

Be sure to ask your friends and neighbors for recommendations. Listen closely to their feedback, as other parents are a large part of what turns a day-care center into a community.

Communicating with the Caregiver

In an ideal situation, your child will become close to her caregiver, who will love her and get to know her because of the time they spend together. It behooves you to develop a close relationship with your child's caregiver so that he feels comfortable talking to you about what he's noticed about your child's moods, learning, development, and adjustment.

To establish a good relationship with your child's caregiver, be sure you are warm and friendly in the morning. Tell her how your child's evening and early morning went and if there's anything she needs to be aware of (if your child is tired, for example, or if she was excited about coming to day care that day). Say goodbye to your child warmly and quickly, as prolonged goodbyes are difficult for everyone. At the end of the day, ask your child's caregiver how the day was. Listen to her and thank her for the information so that she is aware of your interest in your child's daily experience and that she knows you value the feedback she provides you.

Communication Styles

Some day-care centers send children home with written descriptions of the day, such as what they ate, how their mood was, and whether they slept. This is very helpful, as it will give you information for your child's evening, as well as something to talk about with her. "So, you ate a banana today? Was it good?" Although your child most likely cannot answer, his caregivers will have talked to him about this, too, and he will appreciate the continuity from day care to home.

For many parents, there is a "payback" time when kids display anger or seem annoyed that the parent is picking them up. It is a display of some resentment for being left while you had "fun" at work. Tell your child how happy you are to see him, but don't expect him to "discuss" his day or show a lot of enthusiasm when you first pick him up. Transitions are difficult for a young child. After a few calm minutes or a half-hour, he'll be comfortable again.

 Fact

If you can tell, or if your child tells you, that she loves her caregiver and wishes she lived with her, she's not saying she doesn't love you. No one will ever replace a mother or father in a child's eyes, but the ability to love freely and happily is a sign of security.

Remember that many people who choose to work with small children are comfortable with and enjoy the company of small children. It's important that they know you value the intimate way they know your children. After all, they are doing the hard and messy work of cleaning and feeding your child.

Babysitter Basics

Some parents feel comfortable taking a few hours for themselves and leaving their children in the care of others, whether that means family, friends, or a paid caretaker. Others go years without leaving their child with anyone. Adults need adult time, when they focus on catering to their own needs. At some point after the first year, there is a good chance that you will need to get out of the house without your child.

You might be worried about leaving your child with someone else, but an hour or two in the care of another grown-up is good for a baby. You may be able to leave your child with a special person in her life, such as a grandparent, aunt, uncle, older sibling, or family friend. In this case, your child will have a chance to bond with someone significant. Also, it's good for your child to get used to spending some time away from you and learning that you will return safe and sound.

Remember that the more confidence you display to your child about separation, the more confident she will feel over time. If you're sad about leaving (and sometimes you will be) keep that feeling to yourself as much as you can. Of course, you can say "I'm going to miss you, but I'm glad you're going to have fun," but keep the strong, visible emotions out of sight. Your child looks to you to clue her in, often with signals you are barely conscious of, on how safe she is and how her day is going to go.

Babysitters must be comfortable changing diapers, feeding a child, and understanding the specific safety needs of one-year-olds, specifically that they need to be watched all the time. If a babysitter is staying for an extended time, such as more than two hours, she must be able to put a baby down for a nap and know what to do if a baby wakes up crying. For this reason, it is sometimes best to use adult babysitters or teenagers who have taken babysitting classes. Many schools and

YMCAs offer babysitting classes, which are helpful because they teach students what to do in an emergency and how to play with a young child. Not all high-school-age kids—the group available for babysitting—are responsible enough to care for a very young child.

Keep in mind that just because someone is a relative or friend doesn't mean she is capable of watching a young child. Critically consider the personality of any babysitter. If someone you love isn't right for the job, simply say that you don't need that person's help, but that you're happy to have a visit. This can be difficult in the case of close relatives, but your baby's safety is more important than an adult's feelings.

Finding the Right Babysitter

It's best to look at the time you will use a babysitter as a special, beneficial time for your child. Think of the time of day when you need help—is it early afternoon, when your baby will be awake, or in the evening, when she'll need someone to feed her and put her to sleep? Then think of how to make the most of that time. For example, if it's a time when your baby is usually awake, you might want to ask someone who likes to play rather than someone who finds young children tiring.

You'll also want to make sure that your babysitter can be relied upon to show up at the correct time and not need to leave early. To do this, ask potential babysitters for references. Be sure to call and talk to the parents of other children she has cared for.

Also, before you hire her, ask your sitter if she's been around one-year-olds to be sure she's comfortable changing diapers and feeding babies. Set up appointments to have her watch your one-year-old with you at the house to make sure she is timely and interacts well with your child.

If your baby isn't familiar with your sitter, have her come over one time before you're actually going out and let her stay for an hour with you in the house. You don't have to hover over them, but make sure they seem happy together. If your child is suffering from separation anxiety, make sure the baby-sitter can deal with the child's crying without becoming upset herself. She should be able to try various distractions to entice your child into interaction.

 Essential

> Make your sitter feel comfortable in your home. Have food in the house and show her how to use the television. While it's true that she's working, you'll want her to feel relaxed. If there's something you don't want her to do—like use your computer, talk on the phone, or have friends over—make sure you tell her that.

Finally, be sure you are comfortable talking to your sitter about what you expect and how you want her to treat your child. Let her know that you will ask her some information after she sits, such as how your child was, what she ate, if she slept, and how her mood was.

Asking the sitter these questions will tell you two things: first, of course, whether your baby had any troubles, and second, whether your sitter was paying attention and bonded with your baby.

Information to Leave for Your Babysitter

When your sitter arrives, give her a minute or two to say hello to your baby. If your child is nervous about being left, be especially warm and friendly with the sitter. You should feel free to say, "Dylan is feeling a little nervous about my leaving, so I told him that you would be here for a couple of hours. He would really like to play with his blocks and have you read a story to him." Acknowledging your child's feelings and letting your babysitter know them will allow him to see that there's nothing to be shy about and that you and the babysitter want to help him together.

Then walk the sitter through the house, showing her your child's room, the toys, and where to find whatever she'll need in the kitchen. Show her, too, where the phones are. Leave a list of phone numbers, including where you'll be, your cell phone number, your house number (she may need to give it to someone), and the numbers for the police and fire department, and a friend or neighbor she can call if she needs something.

If you plan to call when you're out, let her know, and if you want her to answer the phone whenever it rings, tell her that, too. Ask if she has any questions. Then, say goodbye to your child. Don't linger or drag out your leaving.

When you return, check on your baby before the sitter leaves. Be sure to find out how their time together was, and ask if there's anything she would need if she were to come again.

Remember, you are your sitter's boss, so she'll want what anyone wants while they're at work: respect, support, acknowledgment, decent pay, and direction.

Eating Out

You know exactly what the fear is. You're out with your spouse, a friend, or your family, your baby in your arms, and suddenly, your little dreamboat turns into The Baby Who's Never Acted This Way Before. She'll cry, she'll make a mess, or she'll just be completely unable to sit still.

Babies and the sophisticated dining experience are not natural companions. On the other hand, one-year-olds love going to family-friendly restaurants, and parents may appreciate the experience, too, as long as they have the capacity to let disaster roll off their backs.

Realistic Expectations

The majority of restaurants weren't designed for one-year-old guests. Be realistic about which restaurants and restaurant guests will want to share their space with a one-year-old and how much time in a restaurant your baby can handle. Be sure you tell your dining companions how much time you and your baby can comfortably spend at the table so that you're not stuck with someone who lingers too long after a meal.

If you don't know the restaurant you are going to, call ahead to find out if they have highchairs. If they don't, change venues. Also, try to get a sense of how "grown-up" the restaurant is. During your phone call to the restaurant, you might ask if children are often there for dinner. If you have to make reservations, tell them you are bringing a child; the host's response will let you know how helpful they will be to you and your family.

You want a restaurant with fairly speedy service, as one-year-olds should only be there for an hour at most. When you go, bring along the following:

- A few toys
- Food for your baby
- A change of clothes for your baby
- Diapers and a cloth or mat for changing

In many big cities, there are close-to-upscale restaurants that welcome young children. Ask friends with children or search online for places that give children pizza dough to pound or crayons they can use to write and draw on the paper table cover. Some places even have Cheerios right on the menu. The best part about these restaurants is that they also have grown-up food that you'll enjoy.

Restaurant Etiquette

You certainly have the right to take your child to most public places. At the same time, you know that your one-year-old is not capable of knowing the right way to behave in a fancy restaurant. Although she may do just beautifully while you and your companions dine, rest assured that it is not because she knows her manners. You just got lucky.

If your child behaves like most one-year-olds—babbling, trying to move around, and banging things on the table (this is learning for a one-year-old, remember)—while you're out, be sure no one around you is bothered excessively. More importantly, stay calm with your child and realize that she is having fun, not trying to be rude. Before you spend too much time trying to shush or ignore your child, realize that she will not change in these few minutes and she should not be expected to act older than her age. Young children don't understand the concept behind manners. They want to explore and have fun in their own one-year-old way (walking around, playing, touching everything), so it's best to realize that her behavior will be okay in a very casual setting (usually a restaurant that actually encourages children to come in), but not a formal one.

 Alert!

> Sometimes the problem baby isn't yours—it's one you're with. If that's the case, reassure the mother that you've gone through this and that she should feel free to do what she needs to (take her baby outside for a moment or leave) in order to be comfortable. The most important thing for any mom is that she not be overly stressed.

Everyone has their own sense of what behavior is acceptable and how far they feel their children can go before it's time to either leave the restaurant or face the stares of fellow diners. Some parents need the night out and the cooked meal more than they need to make the strangers at nearby tables happy. Your child will be oblivious to the way her noise is affecting everyone around you. However, she will not be oblivious to your growing tension and self-consciousness (if you feel it). To avoid ruining your dinner, you might discuss a game plan ahead of time with the other adults in your party. Who is up for taking your child for a short walk outside before the meal arrives? Who wants to sit next to her during the meal to help her with her food and to stay quiet? Some adults really want to eat in peace and will not want to be responsible for any children accompanying them. Discussing these things ahead of time will keep everyone at the table from getting frustrated or irritated with each other.

If your child is crying uncontrollably or having a tantrum, go outside for a minute or pay the check and leave. It really isn't fair to other diners, and they definitely don't want to see you or your child struggling with bad behavior. The manager of the restaurant has a right to expect good behavior on the part of his visitors, and he may pay a price in business if diners near you are afraid to come back because they think crying children are a part of the dining experience at this particular restaurant. But don't make this unsettling experience the fault of your one-year-old. Good restaurant behavior is not a typical developmental expectation that is appropriate for this age.

You can begin to teach your child basic table manners, such as taking small bites and using a napkin. By the time she turns two, she will be able to understand how to lower her voice, know not to throw things on the floor, and to sit still for a few minutes at a time when asked.

Remember, you can always ask for the check and leave a restaurant sooner rather than later. Take heart—like most things about your one-year-old, chances are the next time you take your child out, she'll behave completely differently.

Chapter 4

Family Life

Families may include children from previous marriages with different last names, adopted children of different ethnic backgrounds, or a home with one parent. No matter what individuals make up a family, the happiest families all offer love, support, and independence for each member. In this chapter you'll learn more about how to deal with the issues that families sometimes struggle with, such as favoritism and sibling rivalry. You'll learn the skills adults need—patience, routines, and realistic expectations—to help create happy families.

Bonding

What makes a family? Each family would most likely answer that differently. For some, it is sharing a deep religious faith and working toward a common goal in that faith; for others, it means having fun and sharing a love of sports or being outdoors. Still others bond not by similarities but by communication. Even though each member of the family may enjoy different activities, the family comes together at certain times, whether it's dinner every night or holidays around the table, and talks about their interests or jobs.

Regardless of what dynamic your family embraces, sharing and communication are crucial to its success. Two other very important words that help describe a family are support and acceptance. Your one-year-old will bond with you and your family because you take care of him, but this will also happen as he experiences the fruit of your family's love for each member. Hearing laughter, seeing warmth and love, being touched consistently and sweetly, being listened and responded to, and being fed are all ways in which we bond as family.

Bringing a baby into the world and choosing to care for him turns one person into a family, but it can also turn a couple into a family or a larger group into a family. A baby begins to learn who his family is and how the individuals in a family should behave long before he is able to speak. He knows his family members' voices and faces, and he responds positively to both.

Showing Affection

Touch is a sense that many of us take for granted. We learn how to speak with babies so that their language skills will improve, and we learn how to play games with babies so that their motor skills will develop, but many of us don't realize that a loving touch stimulates growth and serenity in babies.

Many Western mothers have been taught that touching their babies too much will spoil or "baby" them, but in reality, touching creates a strong, intimate, and secure bond between family members. You should feel free to carry your baby, sleep with your baby, and cuddle your baby as much as both of you want.

 Fact

Baby massage has been shown to reduce stress crying and promote sleep in young children. You can get DVDs and books specifically on the topic, but if your child is crying or having trouble sleeping, try patting or rubbing your baby's back while talking to her. This touch, along with your presence, will help her relax and will bring you closer.

If your baby seems fussy or unhappy in his stroller, consider carrying him for a few minutes (or as long as is comfortable, depending on his size), or sit down and put him on your lap. When you walk with him, hold his hand, and when you talk with him, bend down and look into his eyes.

While it often seems difficult to do at the time, if you and your child are having a difficult moment, try to take a deep breath and touch your child. This is especially true when a child is having a tantrum. In fact, many therapists and parents recommend holding your child from behind, gently, so that he'll relax into your body. To do this, get down to your knees or sit down on the floor so that you are at your child's height and behind him. Without using force, wrap your arms around your child, bringing his arms around his body (almost as if he's giving himself a hug), and hold him in this position. Let him feel you breathe deeply and evenly; this will actually encourage him to breathe slowly and calmly without your even having to tell him to. Your physical closeness, your breathing, and your calmness will encourage your child to calm down, too.

That kind of physical connection will soothe you, too. The power of touch is not limited to babies and young children. It relaxes and calms people of all ages, bonding them to each other.

Family Activities

An afternoon at the zoo, a morning spent running errands, special holiday dinners—these times make a family, when everyone is pitching in with one another. Parents often want to run errands without their children because it's easier to do anything without having to deal with car seats, strollers, and a toddling fifteen-month-old trying to negotiate steps and revolving doors. But every moment you spend with your child, from the most mundane to the most extraordinary, gives her a sense of inclusion in the family.

Finding or creating activities for your family to do together is a wonderful way to bond. Some families share a love of a certain team and sport, while others spend certain days of the week together, such as Saturday, without interruptions or inviting others along for the ride.

If you want to plan special family activities, first take into consideration the youngest child involved. Plan the day around his needs, such as naps, feeding schedules, and diaper-changing stops. Then consider other important needs: time and places to crawl (or toddle around), and the need to make lots of noise. In other words, you shouldn't expect your one-year-old to enjoy the opera or ballet.

 Essential

"Quality versus quantity" was the debate in the late 1980s and early 1990s, as women balanced motherhood with their careers. Children and parents need both types of time together in order to feel close. Quantity doesn't have to be twenty hours a day, but it should be four to five hours of nonsleeping time on most days, at the least.

Some exciting family outings that work for children and adults include going to places like these:

- The bookstore (with a café and places for kids to play)
- A science museum with kid-friendly exhibits
- The aquarium
- The zoo
- The park
- Sculpture gardens
- An on-site outdoor museum, such as those featuring old ships or airplanes
- Outdoor music concerts

Finally, be loose about your schedule and the itinerary. It's hard for children—and the other adults, for that matter—if they feel too much time pressure. While adults are often used to sticking to their plans, children are easily sidetracked by the most mundane things, such as the bugs on the sidewalk in front of the museum or the steps going from one part of the park to another.

It's best for everyone if you not only let these moments happen but enjoy them as well. Children are curious about these things for a very short time. In a few years, your child will be running off faster than you want him to (although he may be running around more than you want him to this year, too!).

Favoritism

Parents are people, too. They have likes and dislikes, preferences and opinions. When one or two children come along, parents not only have to love their children, but they also have to get to know them. And not all children are compatible with their parents. Great dramas and great comedies alike have come from family situations in which a child doesn't fit in with her family (such as an artist in a world of corporate types, or a child who doesn't like books in a family of readers).

Parents want not only to love but also to *like* their children. They can often see the good in a child, no matter how different she may be from them. For example, even parents who don't like sports usually attend their children's games. Parents often end up appreciating what their children love, which helps make them closer as a family.

Some parents bond easily with one or two of their children but find it difficult to connect with others. If this happens to you, it's important not to blame either yourself or your child for the situation. It's also important that you acknowledge your feelings of disconnection and face them; this will allow you to work through your feelings and work to find a way to connect to your child. Denying feelings and avoiding dealing with them will not help you or your child. If you don't find a way to deal with the issue and overcome these feelings, she will most likely notice them on her own, even at a young age.

 Alert!

Research has shown that people often disfavor children who show traits that those people dislike within themselves. If that is the case, try to show your child the love and support you wish you had received. It is important to support and value the positive attributes in your children, even if you tend to conflict with them.

Of course, if you feel this way, you shouldn't discuss the issue with your child. Instead, acknowledge your feelings to yourself (and your partner or a friend you feel you can trust), and try to work through them. It is usually fairly easy to find likable traits and things to appreciate in any child. If, for example, you wish your child weren't so shy, try to appreciate how quiet and calm she can be. If you wish your child weren't so dramatic, consider playing pretend games to enjoy that aspect of her personality.

When Kids Feel Slighted

Children are the authorities on favoritism. Even if you don't feel it, they know when you're showing it. At the age of one, your child won't be able to say he feels jealous, but he can show his feelings in other ways, such as by coming over to you if you're with another child, pulling your arm, or making a fuss to get your attention.

Research has shown that children, whether favored or disfavored, seem to pick up on the opinions of their parents. So don't think that your feelings aren't transparent. Show your children equal amounts of love and support based on their positive traits, and recognize each child's value.

Reassure your child that you love him and want to pay attention to him, even if he isn't able to tell you about his feelings. Don't ignore or minimize these feelings; at the age of one, your child doesn't yet know that you have enough love for everyone in your life. Until about age four or five, he will believe that the world revolves around him, and it's scary if his main source of reassurance seems to love someone else more.

Sibling Relationships and Rivalry

Chances are that if your one-year-old has a sibling, he or she is older, and any issues of sibling rivalry stem from the older child. One-year-olds in general tend to adore older children (in fact, most children do). Any issues that come up will most likely result from the older child's feeling bored by the crying or feeling threatened or bothered because the one-year-old requires so much parental time and attention.

If your older child is having trouble getting used to her younger sibling, remember that she remembers life without the baby and there are moments when she probably wishes she had you all to herself. Your older child will appreciate you making the time to nourish your relationship with her as much as you nourish the relationships of your expanded family. Some routines that you used to have with your older child, such as reading to her at bedtime or making her a special breakfast, should continue for her peace of mind.

 Essential

If you are close to your siblings, or if you dreamed of having close sibling relationships, you may have expectations for a close relationship developing among your children. But things are almost certain not to be perfect all of the time. The more you let your children find their own connection, the more likely it will be authentic and rich.

The most important thing you need to know is that your kids want you to settle their arguments for them, whether it is in their favor or not. They just want you to be involved because it is a way for them to control you. "Let's watch Mom lose it while we fight," they might as well be saying. "Isn't it a wonder what power and control we have over her?"

Allow some low-level bickering, as it is natural for kids to be competitive and have conflict. If it gets out of hand, separate them with words or physically, if necessary, but don't say anything or pass judgment. Do not get involved verbally or emotionally. If kids get an emotional rise out of you, they win, and the drama will certainly be repeated.

Brothers and sisters fight. Even when they are best friends, or maybe even *because* they are best friends, the need to share toys, parents, and space, along with their age differences (or closeness), sets the relationship up for friction as well as connection, support, and fun. It's important to remember that your children's relationship is just that: your children's relationship. You cannot create it or control it. You can help them with it and set boundaries and guidelines, such as "We don't hit" and "We help each other," but you cannot make them like each other, have things in common, or want to be close.

Even so, chances are that if you leave them to their own devices, your children will find a relationship that works for them. And when they get along, make sure you let them know that you appreciate their good behavior.

Spacing Children

If your one-year-old is your first child, you might be wondering if and when you should have your next baby. Discuss this with your partner, but there's something you should keep in mind. You need to give yourselves some time to let your mind change because very often the desire to have another child is based on the mood and behavior of your first child. Is he being especially cute? Let's have another one! Is he being difficult today? Maybe it's time to stop now.

The most important thing is that you and your partner discuss what would work best for each of you, both of you as a couple, and for your child.

 Question

> **I can't wait to have another baby, but my husband is hesitant. What can I do?**
> Ask your husband for details about his concerns. Is he worried about money? His ability to cope with two children? His opinion is likely based on his desire to keep your family happy and healthy, so if you listen to him with that in mind, there is a better chance that you'll be able to come to a decision together.

Things to consider include the following:

- Schedules
- Money
- Your mutual relationship
- Your current family dynamic
- Goals you have for yourselves
- A new baby's impact on your careers

There is no right answer to the question of when or whether you should have more children. However, it is important that you should know that your body does need time to recover from pregnancy and childbirth, as well as breastfeeding and weaning. The medical community currently recommends that women wait eighteen months between pregnancies. If you want to only have one child in diapers at a time, wait three years. (This way they can still be in school together and be close in age.)

The Family Vacation

The best vacations for families with young children are less about location than about realistic expectations. Your one-year-old will not care that she's zipping down the Autobahn or driving along Highway 1 in California. She will not care if she's on the sand in Florida or Bora Bora. Her experience of a vacation will be very much about the new sensory experiences you expose her to. Save the expensive trips for when she's older and focus on giving you what *you* need. This might be a rest from cleaning, in which case resorts are good. You might want a chance to visit and catch up with friends, a great way to vacation for those with young children—it's cheap! Or you might look forward to getting in some workouts and pampering at a day spa while you visit family, who can be counted on to watch your baby for free.

Like a day trip or a family outing with a toddler, you need to keep your child at the top of the priority list when you plan the details of your family vacation, especially when it comes to packing. Consider each day with his needs in mind, including naps, feeding, and time for play. How many days will you be away? Figure that you'll need two to three changes of clothes a day, as well as toys, a place for him to comfortably sleep, a stroller, food, and a supply of toiletries, including emergency medicines. Some things to take along include the following:

- Diapers, wipes, diaper rash cream
- Extra food
- Bottles (if your baby uses them)
- Pajamas

- Socks
- Hat
- T-shirts
- Another warm layer, like a sweater
- Pain reliever
- Any prescriptions your child uses
- Soap and shampoo
- Toys
- Your baby's comfort item
- Pacifiers if your child uses them
- Books (if you read before bedtime)
- Pediatrician's phone number and insurance information

Don't let the long list of things to bring with you on a trip dissuade you from traveling. It's good to teach your child how to travel and to expose her to lots of experiences so that she feels at home in the world. The keys to a successful journey are organization and a spirit of adventure, as well as the ability to roll with the punches.

Just as you do when planning to eat out in a group, be sure the people you are traveling with have realistic expectations about what a day (or a week) with a one-year-old is like. Your friends will appreciate your explaining, in advance, how much time you'll have for partying and how much time you plan to spend parenting so that no one is surprised by the trip's itinerary.

Fathers

Someone once said that the problem with parenting today is that there is no right resolution to the most common problem of perception: Fathers think they don't get enough credit for all the ways in which they help, especially in comparison to how much their own fathers did, and mothers complain fathers don't do enough. The problem? They are both right.

Fathers of one-year-olds are usually happy with their newly mobile children, who now interact with words and expressions and are more able to play games and have the kind of fun that adults also enjoy. Likewise, it's often easier to leave a one-year-old with a dad than it was when the baby was younger, given that one-year-olds can eat solid food and are not dependent on the breast for nourishment. Also, one-year-olds are not only more able to play, but they will seek out people who like to interact with them more than infants and younger babies are able to.

Dads are famous for playing a little more actively with babies than moms do—throwing them up in the air, knocking them over onto pillows or the bed (one-year-olds love this), and roughhousing on the floor. This kind of play is stimulating and fun to a child who is starting to enjoy his locomotion. If it doesn't come naturally to them, fathers should be encouraged to get on the floor with their children and play at their level. Rolling balls, twirling them around, and playing horsey are all ways children learn to have fun.

To the mother, it can seem as though Daddy gets the fun stuff while she gets stuck with the work. If this describes your situation, tell him how you feel and ask for a switch, even if it's just for a day. It's good for children to see that Dad can feed them and clean them and that Mom likes to play, too. It's helpful for fathers to have a firsthand experience of what moms do, and most moms can use a break every once in a while.

Parents need to make sure that rules—especially the most important ones—are treated and respected consistently between them. This becomes an issue if one parent's approach causes child behavior difficulties for the other parent. So if your partner is getting your child riled up before bed and making bath time difficult for you, explain the problem using "I" terms rather than "you" terms. For example, you could say, "I'm having trouble getting the kids to relax after you play with them. Can I ask you to try to calm them down before bath time?" This works better than "You always get them agitated!" which can sound accusatory and make the other person defensive. Work together to find solutions that work for you and your children.

Your Marriage or Relationship

Any third (or four or fifth) person entering into a relationship is bound to change it. And it takes people a while to negotiate change. Even though it's been a year since you gave birth and welcomed your baby into your home, chances are you and your partner are still figuring out your schedules, your responsibilities and roles, your talents, and your weaknesses as parent and as partners with children.

If all has gone well, you and your partner have been to talk with, support, and love each other through this whole new life. Even in the best-case scenario, chances are that there were at least one or two moments of disconnect, when the two of you found yourselves frustrated, confused, and possibly angry.

So how can two people respond differently to parenthood and still maintain a relationship? The secret is to address the situation as coworkers rather than as just romantic partners.

First, both of you should feel free to explain how you feel. At the same time, you should each do your best to accept the reality of the other person's feelings. Be very clear about expressing your needs in "I" sentences. For example, say, "I need help in the morning" as opposed to "You aren't helping me enough." Then, work to make sure you and your partner are each other's best allies. If one of you needs help, the other steps in. And vice versa.

 ## Essential

> Even though you and your partner fell in love and had children, it doesn't mean that you will parent the same way or agree on parenting all the time. It doesn't mean your partner is wrong, just different. By appreciating your parenting styles, you will teach your children that you have respect for each other, despite your differences.

Don't let your relationship as parents usurp your relationship as lovers, partners, and friends. Both roles are important, and their success is interdependent. Dating, romance, long nights, and late mornings—remember your old life? While there's no denying the presence of your new life, it's important to remember that while you are parents now, you are also still partners in an adult relationship. If you find yourself feeling frustrated by parenting, give yourself a little vacation by going on a date, paying attention to yourself, or having an intimate moment that focuses on you, not your baby.

Stay-at-Home Dads

It's been thirty years since the women's revolution changed not only women's roles but men's as well. If Dad is the one who stays home with your child, you must both accept that it is his job to be the primary caregiver, at least while Mom is at work, and that Mom is not his boss.

A few issues tend to crop up with the working mom/stay-at-home dad scenario. First, it still isn't that common. You will both have to negotiate this set-up with each other as support, rather than the rest of the world. Second, you may have come to this arrangement by circumstance rather than preference, so you might have lingering feelings and thoughts about each other's roles and how the situation came about.

If you find yourself in this situation, whether by planning or surprise, you'll first need to be sure you keep the lines of communication open. You should both do all you can to discuss any issue that comes up, no matter how uncomfortable or awkward—even if it's feelings that you are scared to admit, such as the mother's fear that her child will love his father more. Honesty is really the only policy that works in marriage and parenting.

As with all issues that require good communication, remember to use mostly "I" statements. For example, say "I feel worried when I think you didn't give the baby a nap" as opposed to "You don't make sure the baby naps." Also, be specific about your concern. The issue here is naps, rather than "You don't take care of the baby." If you see your spouse doing something that helps you feel more secure, let him or her know. Remember, this is a new job for both of you. Both of you would appreciate support and praise as much as anyone would on the job.

 Fact

Good communication skills require both honesty and the ability to listen well. As in all your relationships, communication with your partner is key. If both people feel accepted and heard, it's more likely they will be able to work together to handle the realities of family life.

The good news is that men and women who choose to find their own solutions to the day-to-day issues of caretaking, finances, and the creation of a family are, hopefully, putting their children's needs before the world's expectations.

Divorce and Your One-Year-Old

Parenthood is not a guarantee that a marriage or relationship will stay together. Of course, few parents are happy about a breakup, especially when one or more young children are involved, but that doesn't mean divorce doesn't happen. According to results of the 2000 census, 27 percent of U.S. children live in households with only one parent.

According to divorce and family experts, children of "peaceful" divorces experience less stress both as children and as adults. They also do better in school and in their own intimate relationships than those children who live in situations with continued conflict.

When there is too much conflict in a marriage, people shouldn't stay together for the sake of the kids. Research has shown that parents who put their children's needs first and who take responsibility for their actions, behaving responsibly and in an adult manner (no name-calling, blaming, or violence), before and during divorce are more able to be good parents. No matter what your marital status, you should work toward peaceful solutions of conflict. This means that your one-year-old should not witness intense fighting or arguments, should not be kept awake by yelling, and should never be scared by your behavior.

If you find that you and your spouse cannot resolve issues in a peaceful manner, you might try going to a therapist on your own or seeing a domestic violence counselor to learn how to create a more peaceful living environment. Changing your behavior and your relationship habits is not easy and requires true effort. But keep in mind that your child will behave as you do, not only when he is an adult but soon. If you don't want him to yell, hit, or have tantrums, you need to learn how to model good behavior. Counseling and therapy are the best ways to do this.

If your spouse is incapable of reducing conflict, you will have to be the bigger person and learn how to reduce conflict on your own. You will set a great example for your child on how to behave and how to protect yourself from a bully.

No matter what the situation, you need to remember that your child has a right and a need to love each parent, and to likewise judge each parent for himself. You don't have to tell your child what you think of your ex; you only need to behave with honor and integrity. Your child will form his own opinion.

If you can, try to communicate about rules with your ex. Children need consistency with bedtime, diet, and naptimes, at the very least. After that, recognize that there may be some differences between households. Mom may cook at home while Dad always orders out. Many of these differences may be okay. Kids can learn which rules differ from house to house and respect them.

 Alert!

Don't battle for your children's favor by giving in to all their desires. Children get spoiled this way. They get wise to this battle and use your attitude to get their way. Then they get confused when rules need to be enforced by the other parent.

Your Feelings and Behavior

One of the most important things a grownup needs to learn is that feelings and behavior are not one and the same. Although you may be feeling sad, depressed, scared, and worried, rest assured that you can still care for your child. Be honest about your feelings. It's all right to say, "I'm sad" without going into too many details. Try to be present with your child as much as possible. This will show her that emotions are important, but that you are still there for her. She may cheer you up! Be sure she sees you feeling happy and hopeful, too, so she understands the full range of feelings.

It may seem like a hard thing to do, but there are two rewards in it for you. The first is that you will see how well your little one thrives with your love and affection. More than that, her love and affection will in turn give you strength and happiness during this hard time. Spending time with a one-year-old is a great antidote to sadness.

Remember that you shouldn't take your emotions lightly. Divorce is tough. If your child is in a situation where he spends time in multiple households, you'll need to prioritize everyone's needs, including your own. There will be times when you must take care of your own feelings and emotions before addressing your children's, if only because you won't be able to take care of them if you aren't able to find your sense of strength. If you need support, get to a therapist or counselor so that you can help yourself and your child as well. You need love and support to get through divorce just as much as your child does.

Your Child's Response

Even though your one-year-old will not know anything is officially happening, he will absolutely understand changes in the house, especially if they are accompanied by emotional changes in the behavior of his parents.

If you notice your child's behavior or mood is changing, and you suspect that it is because of a change in your marital status, keep your explanation of the situation very simple: "Daddy and I love you even though we aren't going to live together any more." Don't give your child too much information, and do all you can to keep from blaming or speaking poorly about your ex.

If your ex is behaving in a way that upsets your child, you should acknowledge and deal with that behavior, but only in a way that helps and supports your child. Your motivation should not be to hurt your ex.

 Essential

If your partner is abusive—whether the abuse is verbal, physical, or substance—you and your children are better off without him or her. Abusive people do not change with love, and your children will only begin to believe that this behavior is acceptable. You cannot take good care of your children if you aren't taking good care of yourself.

The best thing you can do is keep your child's routine consistent and his time with both of you light. He is a baby, and his world should be safe and expansive, not stressful.

Special Situations

Many parents have an idea about how many children they would like to have, what family situation they would enjoy best, or whether they would like to adopt children or have their own biological children. No matter how many children you end up with—and what order and sexes that child or children come in—or what family situation is your reality, each situation presents itself with specific joys and challenges.

Twins and Multiples

Twins and other multiples are both easier and more challenging at the age of one than they were as infants. This news is somewhat reassuring, but it's also terrifying. How can it be more challenging?

First, your children are now more active than before, which means they are going in different directions (often at the same time) and needing different things (also often at the same time). Second, their needs may become more individual and therefore more time-consuming. Perhaps your son loves to color and your daughter wants to play with balls. Can you do both at the same time?

If you find yourself overwhelmed with their needs, remember that when it comes to multiples, it takes a village. Find people who will help you out, especially when you want to take your children on outings, when it is almost guaranteed they will run in opposite directions. Also consider finding a regular babysitter or dependable day care so that you can relax alone or so that you can devote time to just one child. If you can, find help with the cleaning and maybe the cooking, too.

 Alert!

Just because they are twins doesn't mean they are the same. Your twins will develop and mature at different rates, including walking and talking. Likewise, they may start to differentiate their likes and dislikes, including foods and activities.

Only Children

During his first year, your only child probably benefited from getting the sole attention of parents and possibly an entire extended family, but one-year-olds may also benefit from getting to know children their own age. Your child will be fascinated by the things other children do.

It's important to get your child used to other children; eventually he will be going to school and learning how to make friends and coexist with other children. Only children may benefit from day care simply because of the group activities. Beginning to learn how to behave with his peers will help your only child develop emotionally as well as intellectually.

The children may not actually "play" together, so don't be worried if their play dates are not ideal. For one-year-olds, it's not really age appropriate to share or to play with others—everything is "mine." Just because you are happy your child has a "friend" doesn't mean that he will be happy, too. As you experiment with play dates, you will learn whether your child is naturally social or prefers to play on his own for now.

Single Parents

Despite the sometimes dire predictions of "experts" who claim that children must have two parents in a house in order to do well in school and in life, research has shown that what a child most needs is the unwavering support and love of one person during childhood. The truth is, the quality of parenting is not based on marital status. A single parent may not have a partner, but she may already have what it takes to be a good parent: the commitment and intention to be one.

Single moms sometime believe that being single is a problem and that the solution is to date and find a father for their child, but your child's first need is your attention and not the sense that something is missing from your lives.

Adoption

If you adopted your baby on or close to her date of birth, chances are you've already read a lot about adoption and infants. But parents who adopt foster children or babies from other countries may find themselves with a one-year-old rather than a newborn.

If that is your situation, recognize that bonding is possible with a child at any age. At the same time, by the age of one, your child will have had time to bond with others or at least to get used to another life. She will need time to get used to new routines, new surroundings, and new people. Don't let fear of not bonding get in the way of the natural progression of adjustment that will occur in your specific adoption situation.

 Essential

> The adjustment period varies from child to child and family to family, based on the adoption situation. As with any new experience and routine, it will take some time for your child to get to know you, to feel safe, and to trust the permanence of his new situation. Every adoption has its own story.

Parents and children tend to first go through a honeymoon period, when everyone feels in love with the new situation. You may give your child lots of gifts and begin to believe that everything will always be perfect. Eventually, as with all situations, experiences, and relationships, there will be a testing phase, when everyone may begin to feel the strain and to test the bonds of the new situation. Getting through this period is important, as this is when true love and real parenting begins. It can take months for a new family to adjust to the rhythms and routines of life together. It often helps parents to attend an adoptive parent support group composed of other families who have adopted a child of about the same age.

If your child has come to you as a one-year-old, do not get rid of all signs of her past. If she's come to you with a favorite toy or blanket, or even pictures of her past life, keep them around. These objects do not mean she will not bond with you. They are a part of her reality, and she will trust you more if you allow her to fully transition from the past to the present.

A newly adopted one-year-old may regress to adjust to the big change in his life. You may have assumed your one-year-old would be walking, or you may have been told that he was toilet-trained (which is a very common promise with children from foreign countries). Instead of feeling disappointed, keep in mind that the stress of change may cause your child to "forget" all he's learned. The more understanding you are about this situation, the more likely it is that your child will assimilate his past with his present.

Financial Issues

By the time your baby is one, you have likely recognized the enormous amount of money it requires to keep your baby clothed, fed, comfortable, and safe. Diapers, formula, food, bottles, clothes, day care—it's a seemingly endless amount of cash. Fortunately, now that you've faced the reality, you are well prepared to adjust your finances for today and plan for the future.

If you struggle with a lack of money, remember that what your child most needs from you isn't toys or gifts but attention, love, and guidance. Try to keep your emotions—especially worry, fear, and anxiety—away from your interactions with your child. This will help her, but it will also remind you that you are valuable to your child because of how you behave and who you are, not because of the money in your wallet.

 Fact

According to the U.S. Department of Agriculture, it will cost a parent approximately $250,000 to raise a child born in 2005 to the age of eighteen. That's a lot of money, considering the average four-person family earns about $35,000 each year in income. Careful budgeting is important to lessen the financial stress a family feels.

If you are worried about money, the first thing you have to do is face the reality of your situation. If you have debt or overwhelming expenses get your papers together and call someone for help. There are counselors and financial planners who will help you organize spreadsheets to document the amount of money coming in and the expenses causing money to go out, so that you can create a budget that will allow you to live within your means and save for the future. (See Appendix C for a sample budget, or go to ✍*www.financialplannernetwork.com* to find a financial planner in your area.)

Having a budget and taking control of your financial life will free up your mind and time so that you can be present for your child. Also, once you learn good financial skills, you will be able to pass them on to her.

Family Pets and Your One-Year-Old

At the age of one, your baby is able to move around on her own, whether by crawling or toddling. That means she can easily corner an animal, making it feel vulnerable, and that in turn means it is unsafe to leave her alone even with an animal you love and trust. Even the most loving, best-trained dog or cat can bite or scratch when it feels threatened or frightened.

If you are considering getting a new pet, you might want to wait until your child is at least three, the minimum age at which she will be old enough to understand the rules of behavior around an animal. If a pet is what your family really wants, be sure you do some research on the animals that are most comfortable around small children.

It's important to remember that your pet, while part of the family, is still an animal. As such, it has learned behaviors that you have taught it as well as instincts that it shouldn't be expected to ignore. The relationship between a child and an animal changes as the child grows up, so you need to pay attention to their interaction at each stage.

Never leave your child alone with any animal. The speed at which your newly walking child can get across the room is the speed at which he can grab a tail or put his face near a food bowl. Keep both your pet and your child safe by watching them and not having unrealistic expectations. They both need to be watched and cared for, as well given the space and security to become friends who respect each other's space.

Chapter 5

Teaching Good Behavior

P arents teach by instruction and by example, although many of the lessons they offer are second nature. When you wipe your child's nose when it's runny, he learns both that you love him and how to take care of himself. The reward is that in a few years you will have a child who knows how to behave, is kind to you and others, and tries his best. Meanwhile, you will have developed a relationship in which your child knows he can rely on you and come to you for more assistance.

Routines

Routines are unspoken lessons you teach your children. Regular bedtimes, mealtimes, baths, and consistent time to play and read stories are very important to young children. The whole course of a day is big and unknown to them, so routines give them something to rely on. These regular events allow them to understand what they can expect during the day. Routines also enable them to begin to understand the ways in which you take care of them.

Parental Benefits

Routines aren't just for your child's benefit. Many parents rely on routines to make sure they don't lose aspects of what their lives were like before they had children. If you used to be someone who went to the gym daily or who looked forward to your monthly book club meeting, you know that you had to plan your schedule around those times and dates. If you want to continue doing those things (and you should pick things to continue) then you'll need to do a little more scheduling, taking into account your child's routines as well as your own.

You can create routines around fun things, such as baths and meals, but also around chores and necessities, just as you do for yourself. Picking up toys before bedtime, washing hands before meals, and letting your child see you do laundry and other tasks allows her to see that routines are part of life.

Creating Safety and Normalcy

The most important events that need to be scheduled are meals and sleeping. Once you get your child into a basic schedule, such as breakfast at 7:00, lunch at 12:00, dinner at 6:00, and bedtime at 7:30, you'll soon see that other events will happen around those main events. There will be naptimes, snacks, and time for diapering and baths.

 Fact

From the age of twelve to twenty-four months, babies sleep ten to fourteen hours within a twenty-four-hour period. They'll eat for fifteen to thirty minutes at a time, and it takes a few minutes to dress and diaper them. This actually leaves a fair amount of time for everything else.

It sounds like a full day already, but the truth is that the more planning and routine you have, the more time you'll have for fun and for your own needs, such as shopping, cleaning, and even relaxing. Without routines, your day would be a disorganized rush of things you had to do immediately, which would create stress for both you and your child. For instance, if you wait until your child is hungry before you feed her, she may be irritable and crying. If you wait until she's overtired to put her down for a nap, she will also be unhappy. If you have a set time at which you do these things, though, your child can learn when to expect them and will feel more relaxed about her own day.

Of course, even the best-laid plans often go awry with a one-year-old. There will be days—and sometimes they will happen in a row—when your daughter won't eat when she's supposed to. Or she will take longer than usual, or she won't be able to sleep. Keeping a flexible schedule is key to maintaining peace of mind—and peace in the house. Use a schedule and routines as the backbones of your day, not as the law.

The more routines you and your daughter can rely on, the less likely you are to have to cope with difficult and unpleasant behavior. Your child will best be able to thrive when the life around her is stable and predictable, rather than out of control and last-minute. If the idea of following the same routine and having the same set of events each day sounds dull, remember that nothing is a dull to a one-year-old because every little thing is a new experience.

Setting Limits

John Lennon once commented in *Rolling Stone* magazine that he and Yoko Ono, his wife, had at first thought it would be good to raise their son Sean without many rules. Like many spirited parents of the sixties and seventies, they thought that rules restricted the emotional growth of children. But Lennon and other parents found that thoughtful and realistic rules are not only necessary to development, they help children thrive. Rules and limits—bedtimes, instructions on behavior, overseeing a child's activities—help a child to feel safe and to understand that life is structured and organized. Limits don't only work for children, either. A parent needs to set them so that life with a one-year-old is not out of control.

The Short Rope Theory

Aside from basic safety issues, one-year-olds don't get into the most serious types of trouble—they don't drink and drive, do drugs, or flunk out of high school—so some parents are tempted to let typical one-year-old behavior slide. Why make a big deal out of biting or hitting? Why worry about her running away from you in a store or at the beach as long as you find her quickly? Everyone has seen those parents who let their kids run across the couch, throw food, and not clean up their toys or clothes. After all, these parents reason, the child is only one, and there is plenty of time to teach her how to behave—later.

But involved parents and developmental experts believe that if you give children less behavioral leeway when they are young, you can eventually give them some more freedom as they get older. If a one-year-old grows to understand that her parents are paying attention and giving her consequences and helpful responses to her behavior, chances are that she will be less likely to be out of control when she is older.

Creating Clear Boundaries

Children like rules and boundaries. While there should always be room for horseplay, joking, and an ease of communication, you should make it clear to your one-year-old that you set the rules and you are the grownup. You can do this by being clear and consistent about the rules, meaning that you'll have to repeat yourself a lot to a one-year-old. You can't just say "Be good." "Be good" is too vague for a one-year-old to understand. You need to be specific, such as "I can't let you climb on the counter because there are hot foods there and you could fall, too." This information is clear.

Good habits will make things easier for everyone later on in life. For example, if your child learns sooner rather than later how to clean up, you won't have to worry about breaking a bad sloppiness habit as he grows older. If you know he won't run away from you in public, you'll have to worry that much less about him as time goes by. As your child gets better at setting boundaries for himself, you'll be able to trust him to make good, safe decisions as he gets older.

Realistic Expectations

You want to go to the movies and you wonder if your one-year-old will sit still. You want to walk through downtown for a few hours. Will your one-year-old stay in her stroller that long? What about eating dinner out, or attending a worship service?

It's important to understand two things about young children. First, it is unrealistic to expect them to behave like grown-ups. Second, but like grown-ups, young children have (good and bad) moods and (good and bad) days. You can tell when a friend is having "one of those days"; similarly, it's important to recognize your child will have times when she just won't want to sit still, behave, or play nicely.

 Essential

If you want to sit with a friend for a few minutes, be sure you have plenty of toys on hand to occupy your child. Keep some of them hidden so that when he gets bored with one, you can surprise him with another. Then hide the first toy. It will be a surprise again in a few minutes.

Realistically, you can expect a child between the ages of twelve and twenty-four months to wait for just a few minutes (less than ten) and can sit still for no more than five to fifteen minutes at a time.

Positive Reinforcement

"Thank you for waiting!" and "Thank you for playing with that toy while I was on the phone" are examples of positive reinforcement, in which your comments are reactions to good and effective behavior, rather than negative reactions ("No!" or "Don't!") to undesired behavior on the part of a child.

Research has shown that parents who use positive reinforcement rather than negative discipline have more secure and well-disciplined children. Children respond best to praise because it gives them confidence and information on what to do and how to behave, rather than what not to do in any given situation. For example, if your child is playing quietly in a restaurant, you might say, "Wow! I really like how nicely you are behaving. It's fun to go out to dinner with you." Praise like that is fun to get and it makes him feel good. As a result, he will be more likely to want to continue that behavior than if you reprimand him for spilling something or for talking loudly. Positive reinforcement feels better to the parent, too, because it is an opportunity to show love to your child rather than to be negative or, in the worst case, angry.

Explaining and then naturally praising good behavior will not inflate your child's ego. Instead, it will teach him—very clearly—what works and what you expect. This will encourage him to strive for your praise, rather than fear your wrath. Then, when you do have to say "no" or "don't," your words will matter and not fall on ears that no longer hear criticism or correction.

The Problem with "Discipline"

Rather than increasing a child's understanding of herself and the world she lives in, traditional discipline, including punishment or hitting, merely enforces power. "I told you to be quiet" instills the fearful desire in a child to stay out of trouble. The alternative is to think ahead and find an opportunity to teach your child how to wait patiently. You might say something like "Let's find a way to stay quiet while we're waiting at the doctor's office" to make that a goal for both of you to attain together.

 Fact

Children, like adults, seek praise. If they don't get praise, they often look for any attention, even if it's negative. The worst thing that can happen to any person, but especially to a child, is to be ignored. Learn a stockpile of praise phrases, such as "Way to go!" or "I like when you [fill in the blank]." Use them sincerely and appropriately.

Another problem with traditional discipline is that punishment and other negative-consequence techniques are often random and inconsistent. A parent tends to react emotionally to a negative situation rather than calmly offer guidance on behavior or offer alternatives when a one-year-old is bored or unhappy. Likewise, the punishment (yelling, hitting, or roughly pulling a child) often doesn't fit the crime, given that the natural behavior of a one-year-old (being fussy, not being able to sit still, listen, or share) is not really misbehavior. Even worse, sometimes the crime isn't explained. With traditional punishment, children are told they are wrong or bad rather than having their behavior corrected. Describe exactly what behavior needs to stop ("Please stop kicking the seat in front of you") instead of making negative judgment statements ("You're so bad!"). An effective way to stop negative behavior is to change your child's focus, and therefore her actions, by giving her something to play with or another activity to be interested in.

Temper Tantrums

Tantrums are more likely to happen as your child approaches the age of two. Before then, your child is still thrilled with his newfound freedom. He is not yet completely conscious of his frustration with the limits of his body or with his inability to do whatever he wants at any given time. Temper tantrums tend to occur when a child wants to do something that he isn't able to do because of physical limits or the rules of the family. Early in this year, he will be easily distracted from something that upsets him. Later on, he will try out his behavior to see what works—that is, what he can do to get what he wants.

You will be surprised when your child has his first tantrum—which may involve yelling, screaming, hitting, punching, or standing still and not moving no matter what. But you can rest assured: Tantrums are not a sign that your child is bad or out of control, and they don't mean that something is wrong with your child or that this behavior will continue indefinitely.

They are a natural part of development. Most children have a few of them early in their lives. When parents respond appropriately—calmly and in a detached manner—the child learns that throwing a fit is not effective. As a result, he will learn other, more positive behavior to help him get what he wants. In short, keep in mind that you aren't a bad parent because your child has a tantrum, and they won't last forever.

Tantrums are scary to the child who is having one because the experience makes the child feel out of control. You can help by explaining what's going on; even that distance from their behavior might help them detach from it. Remain calm, and tell your child that he can stop behaving that way if he wants to. It will take a few times for him to hear you, but eventually he will.

Tantrums are about two things: emotions and behavior. But even with an understanding of what's going on, you cannot control how a person—even a young child—behaves. The more you try to control his behavior, the more he has to be upset about. Even though it's difficult, remember that this behavior will go away over time as your child learns more effective ways to handle himself.

Frustration Without Language

Sometimes tantrums occur when a child is unable to explain why she is upset or angry. For example, you might take a toy away and she might react with anger. Given that she can't verbalize her feelings, she may resort to means of communication that are available to her, such as hitting or biting. In a moment like that, it is easy to see what happened. Simply say, "I know you're angry, but I don't want you to hurt yourself.

And here's something else you can do that's just as fun, but not dangerous. When you're ready, I can play with you."

Eventually, your child will see that her behavior isn't helping to achieve her goal of getting her toy back, but that it is keeping her from doing something else.

Safety During a Tantrum

Children rarely hurt themselves when they have a tantrum. They may try head banging or hitting or biting themselves or pulling their own hair. Don't be alarmed if your child tries these tactics. He is seeking attention. The less you try to control this behavior by saying "Don't do that!" the better off you'll be.

 Essential

Tantrums are stressful to parents, too. If you can, remain calm and detached during the tantrum, then allow yourself a few minutes to walk away afterward. Breathe deeply, call a friend, or turn on some music to center yourself.

Through trial and error, your child will find some behaviors to use when he doesn't get his way. Temper tantrums are one set of these behaviors. They come on, but if the response he gets is minimal or ineffective, he will try something else.

Hitting and Biting

Before they learn how to understand themselves and the world, and how to communicate, children try different behaviors to get what they want and express themselves. They may try biting and/or hitting as part of their trial-and-error behavior efforts. This is not a sign of an aggressive personality; rather, aggressive actions are usually the result of feeling threatened ("He took my toy!") and not having the ability to identify, communicate, and handle the feeling. Without those abilities, the child responds in the same way an adult would, with raw emotion such as crying, yelling, hitting, biting, or running away.

Your first response to hitting and biting might be similar to your child's—instinct might take over because seeing your child act aggressively is embarrassing or scary. But you need to remember that this is a natural stage of development and that your job is to teach your child something, not to get angry. She has no idea she's doing anything wrong. If you take her away from the situation with a cool correction—that is, without showing emotion—then she will learn that biting and hitting don't work.

Defusing the Situation

If your one-year-old has hit or bitten another child, the first thing to do is make sure the other child is okay. This is important for two reasons. The child who got hurt or scared needs attention most, and your child needs to see you respond compassionately when someone else is hurt or scared in order to eventually model that behavior. Next, tell your child that it's not okay to hit or bite. Point out how his actions have made the other child feel. He will see the cause and effect even if he can't feel the other child's pain.

If you know that a particular thing upset your child, such as arguing over a toy, it is also important to acknowledge his feelings by saying something like "I know that you were upset that Sarah took your toy." Then, suggest what the biter could have done instead: "Next time you can come get me" or "Next time you can ask to share." Even though all of this language might be impossible for the child to understand, it's still important for you to begin responding to issues in a level-headed, thoughtful manner. One day, your child will understand your words completely, so the habit of clear communication is a good one to get into early.

 Question

> **Another child bit my child and the parent didn't do anything. What should I do?**
> First, make sure your child is okay. Acknowledge what happened, then give her something else to do that takes her away from the other child in order to calm the situation. If they begin to play together again, let them. One incident is not enough to label the other child as a biter or to make you afraid of further interactions.

The last step is to find a reasonable consequence that will suit what your child has done. Traditional forms of discipline, such as hitting or spanking, teach your child nothing. Instead, tell him to sit down for a few minutes, which will allow him to make the connection between his behavior and the negative consequence of missing out on the action. (More than a few minutes is too much for a child this age, as he won't remember why he is being forced to sit still.)

Choose another time, when the subject is not so hot, to talk about biting and hitting. For example, you could simply say, "Biting is wrong. It hurts people." Or you could make up a teaching story about it. The point is to let your child know that hitting and biting do happen, especially in the world of a young child, without making his behavior the specific focus of your talk. Most children are biters at one time or another, but almost all of them get bitten, too.

When you notice your child doing the right thing when he's frustrated, show him how proud and happy you are of his behavior. Also try to avoid making a big deal out of aggressive behavior. The more attention drawn to the behavior, the more appealing that behavior becomes to a one-year-old.

Parenting Styles

You may talk to your child as you would to an adult, while your best friend uses baby talk with her baby. You bring your baby everywhere (even to adult parties), but your best friend has a standing date with a babysitter (and her husband!). Is there a right way to parent?

Yes and no. Most parents love their children, have the best intentions, and do the very best they can do. All parents make mistakes, and all parents have their own personalities. At the same time, however, it's not as if anything goes in parenting. History, psychological research, and plain old common sense have taught parents that some practices, such as bullying, teasing, yelling, corporal punishment, inconsistent behavior, harshness, and neglect, are all troublesome and don't pro-duce happy, healthy children. The only way to be a truly "bad" parent is to be either neglectful and uninvolved or abusive. Research has shown that neglect is as bad as direct abuse.

Raising happy, healthy children should be the goal of every parent. Being involved and responsive is ideal. It reassures your children that you *feel* love for them, but that you also *show* them love by being there to listen, talk, play, and comfort.

Permissive Parents

Permissive parenting is a term that describes a situation in which parents respond emotionally to their children's requests for attention but do not set expectations or limits for them. This kind of parenting is best illustrated by the parents of the spoiled children in Roald Dahl's *Charlie and the Chocolate Factory*—the kids watch TV as much as they want, they eat as much as they want, or get as many toys as they want, and at the same time, they aren't expected to live up to their potential to be giving, well-behaved, and industrious.

If at one year of age your child has no routines, you are a permissive parent. That might mean that he doesn't go to bed at the same time every night, but falls asleep whenever. Or his meals might not be balanced because you feed him based on what he will eat. Permissive parents give their children too much freedom. Ironically, this doesn't create strong children who take care of themselves; instead, it creates children who neither know how to take care of their needs nor understand discipline and good behavior. While no one expects a one-year-old to get a job, you can ask your child to help you put clothes in the laundry basket (rather than picking everything up for him) or have him help you clean up his toys.

Children who aren't given boundaries are often out of control, and when parents are faced with the bad behavior, they lose their temper. Children who have been exposed to permissive parenting are more likely to be involved in problem behavior and to perform less well in school; at the same time, they tend to have higher self-esteem, better social skills, and lower levels of depression. They feel good about themselves, even when, perhaps, they aren't doing as well as they could.

 Alert!

> If you feel like you have lost control of your life since your baby was born, try to find parenting help. Parenting classes or parents whose style you admire can help you find your inner strength. Don't just do it for yourself (although you'll be happy you did), do it for your child. Children want parents who are in charge.

Authoritative Parents

Authoritative parents strive to seek a balance between control and empathy. Studies show that these parents help to produce children who are secure, independent, and have a higher degree of self-control. Authoritative parents are clearly the boss and the teacher, but they nevertheless give their children respect, empathy, and some role in making the decisions that affect them. For example, when your child gets dressed in the morning, you might ask her if she wants to wear her green shirt or her striped shirt. The child has input, but you are in control.

Children of authoritative parents feel safe, but they are also confident. These children learn self-control because they don't have too many options; at the same time, they begin to get used to their ability to make decisions.

Authoritarian Parents

Authoritarian parents believe that the parent is the big boss and that children should obey. They believe that they should be in control of their children and that there is one right way to do things—their way. Children of authoritarian parents often feel frightened and don't learn self-reliance or self-control. They are more likely to rebel later in life. In her book *The Everything® Parent's Guide to Tantrums,* Diana Baumrind defines these parents as "high in demandingness, but low in responsiveness." In other words, they have very high expectations for their children, but they don't react to their children's needs and stages in a manner that provides support for their children. These children look to their parents to set an example, but the parents do not provide guidance yet continue to expect their children to behave well. These children have been shown to have weak social skills, low self-esteem, and higher levels of depression.

When You're Overwhelmed

All parents feel overwhelmed at some point. Perhaps you have a lot on your mind, and when your son asks you to play jack-in-the-box for the twentieth time in a row, you yell "No!" Or your daughter is screaming, resisting being put into the car and tensing up so that you can't fasten her into her car seat.

"Stop it!" you scream. Or maybe your son bites you on the arm and you, without thinking and even though you know better, bite his hand. Stories of parents misbehaving always sound horrible when you hear them, but you may sometimes find yourself acting badly before you even know it.

We all lose our tempers sometimes. Some people yell, some get quiet and walk away (which can be scary to a child), and some people hit—but the thing they have in common is that they lose control and act in ways they don't want to.

Don't be embarrassed to share with friends your stories of losing it—as long as they are the kinds of friends who will share their stories, too. You may be embarrassed, but it will reassure you to know that all parents—even ones you consider to be "perfect"—have their moments of distress.

The first thing you need to know is that parents are not doormats; as a parent, you are allowed to have boundaries, too. If your child is really behaving poorly, it is too much to expect that you will be able to deal with it for as long as the bad behavior continues. It's important to recognize that you have limits. Once you know that, you can work to make sure yours aren't stretched too far.

Losing Your Temper

If you start to yell, or you feel like hitting your child, you will probably have a moment when you can stop. So, do that. Take a breath and stop, even if it means walking out of the room or just turning around. Take the time you need to regain your composure and calm down. Then, apologize to your child. Tell her that you're sorry for your behavior, and, more than that, that she isn't responsible for what you did.

If your children are scared because you yelled or because you hit them, try to acknowledge their feelings and talk with them. Validate their experience of what happened. They need to know you are still there for them and that you love them, even if you were angry or behaved inappropriately.

 Essential

> An apology should never include the word "but," as in, "I'm sorry I yelled, but . . ." That isn't really an apology; it is an excuse. Simply say, "I'm sorry I yelled. I shouldn't have done that, and it wasn't your fault."

Giving Yourself a Break

Parents who strive to be perfect, with a clean house, well-behaved children, and the whole family always in a good mood, are more likely to notice when little things go wrong. Their desire to make things perfect means they are more likely to turn those minor issues into major ones. There is no such thing as perfect—overly clean houses can compromise a child's immune system, overly well-behaved children are often afraid to let loose, and good moods are just one side of life, not the whole experience. You might try these tips:

- Hire someone to clean your house when your to-do list seems overwhelming.
- Go to a movie that is entertaining and isn't too serious.
- Have a night out with friends to remind you that you are a grownup.

- Pamper yourself with a day at the spa.
- Turn on some music and dance.
- Rent an exercise video and exercise while your child naps.

Do these things while someone else is watching your child or when he is asleep. Time off from parenting is necessary because it allows you to recharge and get the energy you need to take good care of your child.

Strive for balance and moderation. Give yourself a break so that when you are doing the job of parenting you can be present and enjoy the job. Figure out what you need to take care of yourself. Whether it's enough sleep (a biggie for most people), time to read, a few gym workouts each week, or dinner out every so often, make sure you get it!

Bad Days

You haven't vacuumed in two weeks, you have a fight with your partner, and you need a haircut. Then your child decides to dump his paint set on the floor. And then you lose it. By losing it, you have turned a crummy day into a truly horrible day. Where do you go from here?

It's important to know that just like you, many parents feel these bad times very acutely because they want so much for their children's days to be good and happy. But it is unrealistic to expect that every day of your children's life will be pleasant or that every day of your life as a parent will be easy.

When you've had a few hours—or a few days—of feeling overwhelmed or being stressed, the first thing you need to do is identify the problem. Are you trying to do too much at once? Do you need a break? Is your child going through a difficult phase that you are struggling with? Have you been inside too long, or is something on your mind?

 **Alert!**

> If you don't have much money, taking a break can be difficult. But you can rely on a mental break to help yourself recharge. When your child naps, give yourself a half-hour to sit quietly, dance, or do some sit-ups—whatever your body needs to feel relaxed. Don't immediately clean the house just because you aren't busy parenting.

If you can pinpoint the source of your stress, you will be more likely to be able to fix the problem. If you can't pinpoint the issue, look to find a way to nourish yourself and your relationship with your child. This might mean doing something together, or, if necessary, doing something apart. Remember, even when it comes to children, absence makes the heart grow fonder, and sometimes it is better to just take a break from a situation. You can get a babysitter or ask a family member or friend to step in for a day, and there is a good chance you will have more to offer your children when they need you.

Getting Help

A book like this offers a lot of information on how to develop the skills and confidence you need to be a parent, but sometimes you will need real-life support—a friend to talk to, a babysitter to take over when you need a few hours for yourself, or even a doctor or therapist to talk with if you feel overwhelmed.

Many parents feel embarrassed to ask for help because they think it means something is wrong with their parenting. But, as the famous African proverb says, "It takes a village to raise a child." Years ago, children were raised within large, extended families and even larger communities. These communities benefited not only the children but the adults as well because they offered support and advice. Plus, there was a lot of physical help—if your child was crying and you needed to make dinner, there was always someone around to do one or the other for you.

So, if the idea of asking for help makes you feel worse than getting the help itself, you'll first need to remind yourself that support is good for both you and your child. The less alone and isolated you feel, the better parent you'll be and, at the same time, the more your child will know that there are people around who are invested in him.

What Kind of Help and Whose

Before you actually ask for help, take two things into consideration. First, determine what kind of help you need. Second, find out who can best give you that help. Finally, think about the best possible ways to ask for the help you need.

Do you need time to yourself? Advice? Someone to watch the baby? Someone to talk to? Do you need to spend time with someone who isn't thirteen months old, or do you need a few hours to yourself? Think about what would really help—time alone, the company of a good listener, advice, or someone to make you laugh. Be clear about what would help. Sometimes something as simple as a ten-minute walk around the block without a child (and maybe with a friend) is enough to make you feel much better.

 Fact

> Your family and friends may not realize that you need help, but that doesn't mean they don't want to help you. In fact, grandparents and friends usually feel honored and happy to be given the opportunity to take care of you and the child you all love.

Now you've come to the big second step: Whom should you ask? The best thing to do is figure out who is the most likely to give you the help you need. Some friends are great for babysitting, while others are great for listening. You might want to ask your mother-in-law for advice, while your father-in-law is the person to ask for help moving the baby's bedroom furniture. You'll be more likely to get what you need if you ask the right person.

How to Ask

To ask for help, tell the person you want help from exactly what you need. For example, you might say, "I'm upset because I haven't had any time to rearrange the baby's bedroom furniture. I want to put his art table in the corner and I can't move his crib by myself." Then directly ask for help by saying something like, "I was wondering if you could help me?"

Chances are that your loved one will give you what you need and be happy doing it. Even if the person you ask cannot give you the help you need, that doesn't mean you should give up! Ask the person if there is another time when he can help. You may have to turn to someone else or offer to do a favor for the other person (especially if the other person is also a parent), but you will ultimately find someone to help you. Asking for help is an opportunity to build stronger family relationships and a tight-knit community with friends and other parents.

Chapter 6

Sleep Basics

Your baby might seem most lovable when she is asleep. She isn't putting anything dangerous in her mouth, she isn't crying, and she doesn't need you to watch her. It's heaven. Whether your children sleep with you or in a crib or bed, parents tend to have two basic questions: how to get a child to go to sleep in the first place, and how to keep her asleep once she's snoozing. It is the rare one-year-old who sleeps through the night and doesn't wake up even occasionally for a bottle or for comforting.

Bedtime Routines

Experts now agree that sleep is a habit, a learned phenomenon. Human beings are not born with the ability to fall asleep easily and to sleep soundly. It turns out that children need to be encouraged and taught to fall asleep. You should respond to all crying during the first few months of your child's life, no matter what time it happens. Infants need security and emotional warmth more than anything—and when they cry, they need you. Around her first birthday, you will probably need to teach your child how to go to sleep, which means establishing a routine and a setting that is restful and encourages sleep.

 Fact

Most bedtime routines feature a bath, tooth brushing, changing a diaper and putting on pajamas, then reading a story, and singing a couple of lullabies. This routine is comforting and soothing. If you keep the lights low and your voice soft, your child will naturally begin to feel sleepy.

A routine isn't foolproof, but it's a great habit to get into for many reasons. First, bedtime routines will give you and your family a schedule to work around. Also, since the time after dinner is when your child is winding down and may be cranky, having a routine will give you and your baby something to rely on and look forward to: reading, baths, and cuddling. Bedtime routines are full of warm and loving moments that can often erase the memories of a difficult day.

Some children need to burn off energy before bedtime. If that's true in your house, you might want to incorporate physical exercise into your routine, such as playing Chase Me or Hide and Seek. Even if you are playing actively, turn off the television as you run around. End up in the bathroom or bedroom for washing up, brushing teeth, and diaper changing. If you want, transition from the physical activity to quiet time by telling a story. Then start the reading and lullaby routine, ending with the lights out and a kiss goodnight.

If your child is overtired, it may take a few more minutes than usual to get him to settle down enough to start your routine. You can help soothe him by dimming the lights, turning off the television, and speaking in a soft voice. Try not to respond to your child's behavior in a way that creates a power struggle, and instead let him wind down on his own.

While you will need to create your own bedtime routine based on things like your furniture (will you lie on the bed to read stories or sit in a rocking chair?) and personal taste (music or no music?), here are some examples of good bedtime routines and the situations in which they work.

Sample Bedtime Routine 1

For a child who is already a little sleepy

1. Give your child a bath with a lavender-scented oil, which encourages rest.
2. Turn down the lights.
3. Lie in bed with him or hold him in a rocking chair.
4. Read a short story.
5. Sing a song.

6. Rock him for a few minutes.
7. Put him in his crib or bed and rub his back.
8. Turn off the lights and leave the room.

Sample Bedtime Routine 2

For a child who needs to burn off excess energy

1. Turn off the television. Play some music and play or dance with your child for fifteen minutes.
2. Say, "In five minutes we're getting ready for bed."
3. At the end of five minutes, turn off the music and bring your child into the bathroom and talk softly. Encourage your child to lower his voice.
4. Bathe him.
5. Brush his teeth and put him into his pajamas.
6. Sit or lie with him in his room with the lights dimmed and read a book.
7. Sing a song.
8. Put him in his bed or crib and rub his back.
9. Turn off the lights and let him go to sleep.

Bedtime routines should feature dim lighting, no television, and quiet. Children need to learn how to go to bed and fall asleep, and you can help them get used to the process.

Comfort Items

Blankies, teddy bears, pacifiers—almost all kids have an inanimate object that they don't just love but actually need. It's important not to discourage their use or to make fun of a child for needing a security object. Children use all types of objects as security blankets. Little boys often want to carry a small toy or action figure with them. Little girls might want a doll. You should try to get a second version of this object in case something happens to the first.

Source of Security

These objects do a job and play an important role in a child's development. Their use should be not only respected but appreciated as well. The chosen object gives children a sense of strength and familiarity, feelings that are not natu- rally available to a child at every moment and that all of us need to get through each day. Children need time to develop the inner strength and security that well-adjusted adults have as a matter of course. Before they are able to do that, they use their comfort item as its source.

 Essential

In the *Peanuts* comic strip, Linus takes a lot of heat for suck- ing his thumb and carrying his security blanket around. However, Linus is also one of the wisest *Peanuts* characters. This is a very clear illustration of the fact that the need for a blankie does not make a child a baby.

Most children pick their own security object and are pretty quiet about it, carrying it around from room to room or seek- ing it out when they are tired or unhappy. Once you notice what the object is, you should give it the same respect your child does. He will appreciate this and feel more comfortable with its use. Your child will probably want to hold his blankie when he sleeps, when he is trying to relax (such as sitting on the couch or listening to a story), or when he's upset. Always have it on hand and give it to your child before bed so that he feels safe.

As they get older, children will sometimes endow these special objects with magic powers. A child might think his blanket can hear him when he talks or that he is protected if he puts it around his shoulders. It is not unusual for a child to continue carrying his object of affection for years, to the age of five or six.

Safety Concerns

Most security objects are safe for a one-year-old to bring to bed and sleep with. The exception to this rule is a pacifier: Your child should not suck on one while he sleeps. At the age of one, your child can safely sleep with a blankie or stuffed animal in his bed.

If he brings a blankie with him to bed, make sure after he has fallen asleep that the blankie is not too close to his face or near his head. If he has a stuffed animal, make sure it's somewhere up on the bed and not on the floor (so he can find it if he needs it during the night), but that it, too, isn't too close to his face.

Waking Up at Night

You probably wake up a few times during the night. You briefly open your eyes, register that you have woken up, and close your eyes again. This sequence comes so naturally to you that you probably don't even remember it in the morning.

Young children, however, don't yet know how to easily transition from sleep to waking and back again. It is not unusual for one-year-olds to wake up feeling frightened and to immediately cry out for you. If they really get scared (or if it's early in the morning and the sun is up), they might climb out of their crib and come get you.

 Question

Does day care help a child sleep at night?
Day care usually gets children on a routine that is rarely, if ever, changed, which helps them feel relaxed at bedtime. Day care also provides your one-year-old with constant activity that can tire him out for bed.

It's important to realize that learning how to fall back asleep is as much a process as learning to fall asleep in the first place. See sleep training as part of your job rather than as a nuisance designed to rob you of more sleep. When you teach your child how to sleep, you not only teach him something valuable, but you may be able to go back to the world of grownups who get to sleep through the night!

When your child calls to you at night, don't go to her immediately. First, try calling back to her and saying "Go to sleep. It's still bedtime." Give her a few minutes to settle herself down. If that doesn't work, go in to her. Without turning on the light, say, "It's okay. Go back to sleep. It's not time to wake up yet."

You might tuck her in again, pat her back for a few minutes, and give her a quick kiss or hug, but don't take her out of her crib or bed.

If she cries or gets upset when you try to leave, go back and reassure her again. Remind her that she went to bed a little while ago and she's just as fine now as she was then. If you need to, turn on a song that relaxes her or sing to her for a few seconds so that she is reminded of her bedtime routine. Do all you can though to not encourage waking up. Give her a few minutes to settle herself and then leave.

If this starts to become a nightly routine, you may need to stop getting out of bed and try to calm her simply by calling back to her, "You're okay—go back to sleep." Your child may get used to the attention she's getting and may start doing more and more to get you to pick her up. While it's important for your child to feel secure and comforted, your goal here is to give her some solid sleep time, which is vital to her health.

Many parents teach their children to go to bed at night but bring them into the grownup bed if the child wakes up in the middle of the night. There is nothing inherently wrong with this—it's simply an adaptation of the family bed, which is very common in many cultures (as described in the following section). However, it might be worthwhile trying to teach your child to go back to sleep just so she learns how.

Family Bed

Family bed is a Western term that was coined to describe a practice that is very common in other parts of the world. While in the West it is traditional for families to put children in their own beds, separate from the parents, other cultures see sleep as a communal time. Within the past generation, many Western families have begun adopting this tradition and bringing their young children to sleep with them in the family bed.

Skeptics about this practice tend to have two basic arguments. First, it is hard for them to understand how a couple can continue to be physically intimate if there is a child sleeping there in the same bed. Second, they believe that leaving children alone, particularly during sleep time, is vital to their ability to learn independence and self-reliance.

 Alert!

> If your child is truly scared or has night terrors, meaning he wakes up screaming uncontrollably, you need to comfort him without hesitation. Fear is different than waking up and your child needs to know he is safe and that you are nearby to take care of him.

The answer to the first question is determined by the individual couple. Usually, the child does have a separate place to sleep. Because children usually go to bed before adults, parents put the child to sleep in his own bed, leaving them free to enjoy a little alone time in bed together if they wish. It is also common for the "family bed" to consist of the grownup bed plus a crib or an extension (called a co-sleeper) that is pulled up to the side. Obviously, this arrangement does take thought and planning, as well as the enthusiastic agreement of both parents. It is important to make sure that you do continue to connect as a couple and that having a child in your bed does not lead you to neglect your relationship.

Having babies or young children in your bed also doesn't have to be an either/or proposition. You might choose to let her sleep with you on some nights, but also encourage her to sleep on her own during other nights. Some children, if they know sleeping with you is an option, won't need it as much as others.

As far as the second objection goes, some Western parents—and children—put tremendous value on the intimacy and connectedness they get from sharing sleep. As a consequence, they don't worry about the messages this country sends to parents who sleep with their children (They'll never be independent! They'll never get out of your bed!). The truth is that no matter how much your children enjoy sleeping with you when they are young, they will eventually want privacy and more space. Sooner or later, they will end up sleeping in their own beds.

Transitioning to a Separate Bed

If your child is sleeping in the family bed now, chances are that she has slept there since soon after she was born. You have established a shared sleep routine that accommodates her need for security and comfort as well as your need for privacy and adult alone time. The question now is when you should start thinking about letting her get used to sleeping in her own bed.

There are many opinions on the potential harm and/or benefit that come from independent sleep. Some books raise dire warnings about failing to teach a child how to get through the night alone, while others counsel against giving your child the feeling you have abandoned him. The truth is somewhere in between, at a point that differs for every child and every family. You know your child better than anyone else. Rather than letting yourself be swayed by theories of experts who have never met you or your child, use your own powers of observation to tell you when your child has matured to the point that independent sleep is a bigger benefit than sleep with you.

The answer might turn out to be very practical: As children grow older, they grow more active in their sleep. If your one-year-old kicks and thrashes through the night, he may be resting just fine while you are losing a lot of valuable sleep. If that's the case, it's time for him to move on and let you have your comfortable bed back to yourselves.

Common Sleep Problems

Sleep is an issue for many people. It is often difficult for adults who have trouble sleeping to teach their children how to sleep. If you practice certain routines, both you and your children are more likely to sleep well.

Signs that a child needs more sleep include irritability, falling asleep quickly in the car or if the lights are low during the day, and not being engaged with what's going on around her. One-year-olds need about fifteen hours of sleep in every twenty-four-hour period, which usually means a ten- to twelve-hour sleep period at night, with a long nap during the day.

If your child isn't falling asleep when you want her to, it's possible that she needs to sleep less during the day, be more active during the day, or wake up earlier in the morning. Try to adjust her sleep hours by fifteen minutes each day until she is going to bed when you want her to. If she's going to bed at ten and waking at eight, but you want her to go to bed two hours earlier, then you'll need to wake her fifteen minutes early and put her to bed fifteen minutes early each day. Keep increasing that time by fifteen minutes every day until she's going to bed at the time you want.

If your child wakes up very early, rest assured that this is very common. Most young children have their internal clock set at a more natural rhythm than those of us who stay up reading well past sundown. Be sure her room stays dark until whatever time you are ready for her to get up. You also might want to encourage her to simply come into your bed and go back to sleep. Early mornings together are often just enough cuddling for a family.

Moving to a Bed

At twelve months, it is unlikely that your child will be ready to move into a bed, but he will be more ready as he gets closer to twenty-four months. If your child is climbing out of his crib or is close to the same length as his mattress, he is ready for a bed. You may be nervous that he will roll out of the bed, but it's possible to get bumpers or bars to put around the bed that will prevent this from happening. It is much safer for him to be in a toddler bed than a crib that he can climb out of; the bars of a crib are higher than the edge of a bed, and a fall could be dangerous.

If your child is comfortable in his crib and not trying to escape from it, then you should certainly feel free to let him sleep in it until he is closer to two.

Most children are thrilled to be in a bed, especially if you have outfitted it with nifty sheets covered in something they love (flowers, motorcycles, sports figures, or favorite cartoon characters). To encourage their excitement, set the bed up a few weeks before they will be expected to sleep there each night. Lie down with them, take a nap with them, and then let them take naps there. They just might decide on their own that they'll never go back to their crib again—something that often happens when a child gets excited about a new bed setup.

Common Fears

If your child is nervous about this change, it might be for a few reasons. First, she knows that she will never be in a crib again, and her crib might be a favorite place. Let her say goodbye to it and acknowledge her feelings of attachment.

Some children have to move into a bed because there is a new baby in the house, or because you are moving to a new home altogether. You can always present the bed as her reward for all of these special changes. Most children really are thrilled that they are involved in something special and that the changes aren't just happening around them.

You might also explain to your child that even though she will be sleeping in a bed, she will still be your baby and that you're always going to love her and take care of her no matter where she sleeps. Tell her (and demonstrate) that you will continue your bedtime rituals—the songs, the reading, the bath time—and that you are happy to lie down with her for a few minutes if she would like. She needs to know that the only thing that has changed is the actual bed, not the love and affection you share.

Bed Safety

Bed are generally safe for older babies and younger children, unless you have a child who rolls around a lot and isn't easily awakened. Many children do sleep very deeply. If she can't feel that her arm or leg is dangling off the side, you might need to get rails or a bed that has higher rims.

 Essential

Some parents buy special toddler beds, which are lower to the ground. These cost around $100 and can hold a crib-sized mattress. There is no inherent benefit to these, unless you think your child will be less likely to fall out or that it will make the transition easier. But she won't be able to stay in one of these long, because the mattresses are very small.

At the age of one, your child can sleep with blankets and a small pillow. Many children can cover themselves back up if the blankets fall off. If your child can't, and she's kicking these things off at night, she can still be in a zippered outfit that covers her from her neck to her toes. Just make sure she isn't getting overheated.

Chapter 7

Early Learning

From twelve to twenty-four months, your baby's mind will develop in amazing ways. By the end of his second year, he will be able to identify colors, follow simple instructions, and understand the rhythm of the day and his routines. He will know and appreciate the relationships he has with her family and caregivers—hugging and kissing you as a way to show love. Much of what he learns won't be what you teach him, but what he absorbs and thinks about in his own way.

Brain Connections

Everyone wants their baby to be smart and learn things, but learning does not only mean knowing facts. Especially at one year of age, learning is not a linear process. It is much more of a holistic process, involving all sorts of connections and cross-references that the brain makes as it begins to understand and formulate thoughts about the world it is experiencing. The rounded shape of the brain, in fact, reflects the three-dimensional way cognition and perception work. Smart brains are brains filled with connections—neural pathways and synapses that connect one perception to a thought and then a thought to an idea and then back to another perception and then to another thought. One-year-old brains are making sense of the world. The more things your one-year-old takes in—whether it's words or sensory experiences (such as hugs and playing with toys) and sights and sounds—the more likely she is to develop intellectually as she gets older.

These perceptions, thoughts, and ideas, however, are not really taught, especially during this year of life. At this age, children's "thinking" is less by rote than by experience. For example, if, in the course of a day, you give your child a spoon to bang, sing a song with her, play peek-a-boo, read her a story, and go outside for a walk, she won't just learn about spoons, music, your eyes, a book, and the grass. She will also have thoughts and make connections about those things. For example, she might want to bring the spoon onto the grass and see what it sounds like; she might sing the song while you read her a story; she might play peek-a-boo with another baby she meets. And so on and so on—basic creative connections are what brain development is all about, especially at this age.

 Fact

> One reason it is best to not direct your child's play with learning toys is because creativity comes from free time and the freedom to make thought and idea connections that haven't been directed by a toy, parent, or teacher. Children love this free play, which is why they are more apt to play with a box a toy comes in than the toy itself.

Keep in mind that your baby can get tired from too much stimulation and thinking. Just as you may find it exhausting to work on your taxes or to read a heavy novel, your baby's brain needs to rest when it has seen and considered a lot. One-year-olds need one or two naps a day and a full night's sleep.

Exposure to the World

What makes brain connections happen is exposure, whether to words, nature, people, animals, or products. The more you see and do, the more your brain will have to wrap itself around these new perceptions. Of course, one-year-olds also learn through their relationships with adults and other children. Exposure is not just one-way, it needs to be interactive.

One of the best things you can do for your baby is bring her places. Each new place will give her something to look at and consider. While it may seem easier to run errands yourself or to go out without her, she will thrive intellectually if she has seen and been exposed to many things before she even goes to school.

Talking About the World

When you take your child out into the world, talk to her about everything she is seeing. All of the words you use are also a new type of exposure; in your house, you don't have some of those things to discuss ("See the cows? There are five!" "Look at the pretty flowers! Roses and tulips!")

Your child won't necessarily understand what you're talking about, but she will try to figure out what you're saying—and that, too, encourages brain development. She will look around and try to link your words with what she sees.

By the end of this year, she will also begin pointing things out to you. Noticing the world around her is an important sign of growth, and communicating about it is also significant.

The Grocery Store

It may seem boring to you, but there are few places more stimulating than grocery stores for your one-year-old. Your child will adore getting strapped in for a ride in the cart and looking around. Talk to your child about the store, even about the things that seem over her head, like money, what food you're buying, and the people you see ("Look at that man, he's putting bananas on the shelf!").

Grocery stores are not good places for small children to run around because they can pull down boxes and products that are dangerous. Never let your child ride in the part of the cart meant for groceries, and don't let her reach for anything. She could not only pull something down on herself but also knock the cart over.

 Alert!

> Some children are overwhelmed by the bright lights and loud noises in a grocery store. If that's true of your child, plan your trips to be short and organized. Get in and get out quickly so that she doesn't get irritated by everything going on around her.

Colors

This year your child will start to recognize and differentiate between colors. The grocery store is a wonderful place to introduce your child to colors without making it obvious that you are teaching her something. "Should we get green apples or red apples?" "Do you see the cereal box with the pirate on it? The box is white and the pirate has a black hat."

You can consistently point things out to your child, and she will be intrigued by all that you are saying and showing her. You'll notice that if you hold the bananas or apples next to you and say "yellow" or "apples" (or whatever word you want to say), she'll try to mimic you.

Touching

Another great thing about grocery stores is that they have a lot of things that aren't breakable (like cardboard cereal boxes, fruit, vegetables, packages of cheese or pasta) and that are relatively safe in the hands of a one-year old. You can hand your child things to carry and touch, such as fruit, bread, and small boxes of food. If she tries to take things off the shelves, simply hand her something from your cart to distract her.

If your child is sitting in the front of the cart, you can hand her boxes and packages of food and let her drop them into the cart behind her (make sure it's things that can be dropped, like bread and cereal boxes). She'll enjoy helping you and the actual dropping, too.

Museums

There are parents who would never dream of taking their toddler to a museum, knowing that they are going to yell and run around and try to touch the paintings (unless you're lucky enough to get them to stay in their stroller). But children often get into museums for free, and many museums have play areas and learning rooms specifically designed for children.

Many museums, zoos, aquariums, and other cultural centers have programs that allow you to get passes for an entire family for the year. Sometimes a town or museum system will have programs that get you into many museums throughout the year. Museums are good outings for families, and these programs can be bargains in the long run.

One thing you might want to try before you head to a museum is giving your child a chance to run around outside for a significant amount of time. If she's a little tired when you head in there, she might be content to sit in her stroller and look around for longer than she otherwise would. And even though food is usually forbidden in museums, bottles are usually permitted. Bringing along a bottle or sippy cup can prevent your one-year-old from getting fussy or needing to be removed in order to have a drink.

The secret to museums visits is, once again, realistic expectations. Assume that your child will be manageable for a half-hour to one hour. If that doesn't sound like a lot, rest assured that spending thirty to sixty minutes in a museum will expose your child to an amazing array of new sights and sounds, stimulating her brain.

Aquariums and Zoos

One of the best things about being a parent is that you, too, get to go to wonderful and educational places like aquariums and zoos and can enjoy them with your one-year-old. If you're heading to an exciting place like this, go early or late in the day. Try to avoid lunchtime and the middle of the day, when these places are the most crowded. Your child will be one of the smaller children, and it will be difficult for him to see exhibits (and run around safely) amid lots of other children.

 Fact

At this age, your child may not be able to sit still for the special shows and movies that usually run at museums, aquariums, and zoos. Save your money and take her when she's older. Also, you can assume that your young child will only be interested in what's around her for thirty to sixty minutes.

Bring snacks and a stroller that reclines, if possible, so that your child can nap. This will give you a little more time to walk around and see things on your own. And always remember to bring diapers and wipes (which will help you all keep your hands clean, besides their other uses).

Young children might not always respond positively to the animals in petting zoos. Even small animals, such as goats, can overwhelm a small child, especially if he has food in his hands. Be prepared to let your child keep his distance if he wants. It's better to follow his lead than to force him to "enjoy" the experience.

Real Life

To you, it's as dull as anything, but to your young child, the laundry and all those other chores you find less than entertaining are new and thrilling. Your child will want to take her time exploring the house and the everyday world around you just as much as she'll want to run around a museum or look at the animals in a zoo.

In fact, it will be helpful to both you and your child if you explore the house together. If she wants to take things out of cupboards, help rather than discourage her (take away anything glass or sharp, of course). Don't worry, because, at this age, cleaning up is as fun for your child as making a mess. Have her help you put all of the items back in the cupboard.

Cars and Large Machines

Most children love toy cars because they roll and mimic something children see and experience every day. You can buy inexpensive play rugs that have streets and roads printed on them. These are made to encourage young children to play with their cars and make houses and other buildings in the town printed on the rug.

Train stations, airports, and any other places that feature a form of transportation are exciting to a one-year-old (or even an older child). If you're ever looking for something to do one afternoon, consider just going to your local train station when a train is scheduled to come in. Or, if you can, take a train ride from your town to the next town—have someone meet you at the station, or take the train back. Your child will love this experience.

If your child is ever stressed or bored, bring him outside and let him sit in the front seat of the car with you (don't start it!). He'll love touching the steering wheel and looking out the window. If your child is fascinated with trucks and cars, take him for walks around town where vehicles are parked. Keep him in his stroller, but point out the colors, the wheels, and the noises the vehicles make. This is the kind of outing that a young child loves, even though you're actually just spending time in a parking lot.

Computers

There are numerous computer products on the market that claim to help your child—even a very young child—learn to read, use computers, and do math. However, computer games and even programs that teach skills are no better at improving intelligence or thinking skills than building blocks or banging on cans. At this age, children's brains will grow more if they are stimulated by sensory experiences and free-form play.

Clothes

While you see clothes as practical garments that your child needs to get in and out of (often more than once a day), your child sees an opportunity for playtime. Look! Socks go on and off! Look! I can pull my shirt over my head and no one can see me! (Or so she thinks.) As a parent who needs to get things done, how do you teach your child to not play with her clothes? Think realistically and compromise.

 Essential

> Some children are very particular about the clothes they wear. If your child shows strong preferences, give her limited choices. Don't ask, "What shirt do you want to wear today?" but instead, "Do you want to wear your blue shirt or your pink shirt?"

First, if you know your child enjoys playing with clothes, give her some things to enjoy before you try to get her dressed. Then, if she resists getting dressed even after playing, give her one object to enjoy—a scarf or a hat—while you explain that some of her clothes have to be on and that she needs to wear the clothes you've decided on.

Some children become obsessed with certain items of clothing, wanting to only wear their orange shirt or their pink socks, for example. It's a good idea to indulge this obsession if you can. It's not worth struggling over and it shows them that you encourage their interests. They will become less obsessed the calmer you are about it.

Some children hate getting dressed, and some can't stop fidgeting for long enough to get their clothes on. If clothes are a struggle with your child, don't turn the situation into a daily problem. If you make the mistake of waging a big getting-dressed battle every day, you are letting your one-year-old control the situation. To solve this, figure out what your child wants—does she want to choose her own clothes? Let her. Does she want to play? Set limits, and explain that she can play before and after she gets dressed. Make sure the clothes you choose are very easy for her to get into. Keep your cool, too. It's only clothes, and this is definitely one of those things she will become less interested in over time.

Cleaning

If you're dusting, he'll want to dust. If you're vacuuming, he'll want to play with the vacuum. Children do not see cleaning as a chore. If you do a lot of it, they will think it is something wonderful and they will want to do it, too. Encourage this as much as possible. This is not because you need a little helper (their help may not actually "help") but because they are developing their confidence about growing up. Many of the physical motions of cleaning are also wonderful for their development. Here are some ways your one-year-old can enjoy cleaning with you:

- Dropping clothes in a laundry basket
- Being on the bed while you make it
- Putting toys into a toy chest
- Carrying clean clothes into his room
- Using a rag to dust

Cooking

Young children love to help with cooking. They will enjoy playing in toy kitchens and will want to play with your pots, pans, bowls, and spoons, too. This is, once again, a way in which they can imitate you. It is also a wonderful way for them to develop their fine motor skills—stirring, patting, and rolling are all great for their hands and their hand-eye coordination.

Plastic utensils and cookery are the perfect toys for children this age. Bowls especially lend themselves to creative play, as they can suddenly turn from a bowl to a hat, or from a building block to a house for a doll.

Outside

Most one-year-old children love the outdoors—showers or sunshine, windy or hot—they don't notice the overall weather as much as they notice little things, like grass, snow, and rain. One of the best things you can do for a child is let him explore the outdoors with you. Keep an eye on him, but do your best not to hover—let him touch dirt, flowers, and whatever he sees that is safe. If he picks up something dirty, simply tell him it's not safe and take it away, but don't make him stop exploring.

You'll notice that one-year-olds often don't get far in their explorations. They are like little scientists, stopping very quickly at something and looking at it intently for longer than is interesting to someone (like you) who is already familiar with sand or blades of grass. If you can, try not to rush this inquiry. While grownups often want to show their little ones all there is to see—look at the house, the slide, the beach!—

one-year-olds are often content to examine one thing at very close range.

 Alert!

> While running around barefoot is certainly one of life's pleasures, it is best to save this for your own yard or other private place. A one-year-old does not know to look out for glass or other things that can cut or hurt her, and a bad cut will keep her off her feet for longer than she'd like.

Parks

One of the great things about taking your child to a park is that it's free. And while parents often think one of the best things they can do for their child is buy them educational toys, the truth is that nature is the best teacher of all. Point out the way the clouds change in the sky, the sounds that squirrels make, and the different birds. Let your child feel the bark of a tree and the metal of the benches.

Don't be too disappointed if you've only been at the park fifteen minutes before your one-year-old is ready to pack up and go home. Older kids have the benefit of longer-term memory and associations, and they remember the park as a place where they have a lot of fun. At this age, a child sometimes just isn't in the mood and can't switch gears the way an older child can. A short visit this time doesn't mean she won't enjoy it for longer next time.

You might want to bring some things to a park for your child, such as a big ball (she'll have more space to try to kick and throw it), a blanket (so she can lie down when she's tired), and a snack, as well as something to drink. Be sure she wears a hat and sunscreen.

Your child will most likely want to show you the things she sees and picks up in the park, so enjoy playing the role of student as she points out everything she notices. For example, admire your one-year-old as she picks up a roly-poly without fear, even if she squishes it as she does so. Let her show you a spider as it climbs up the wall. At the age of one, many children are not yet afraid of bugs. If you can, try to refrain from transmitting your fear (if you have one), and encourage this scientific discovery.

Water and Swimming

If you're taking your one-year-old to the beach or a lake, you'll find that he either loves the water or is hesitant to go near it. This might be because he understands that he can't swim, and it might trouble him that he can't see the bottom. (Some children assume they can swim and jump right in.)

If your child is nervous around water, it might not be the actual water but the noise of the waves or the murkiness of the lake that bothers him. You will need to explain the surroundings to him, pointing out the water is clear in your hand and that it's the mud that's dark or that the waves are gentle when they are near you. If you can, sit down with him in the water so that he doesn't feel all alone down there.

No matter how well your child takes to the water, he is unable to swim by himself for any period of time. You must always stand within arm's reach of your baby, preferably with your hands on him or as close to him as possible. It can take just a few seconds for a baby to drown. If you have to jump in or swim over to him, you could be too late. No matter how shallow the water, your baby should also be wearing a life preserver or a supportive flotation device so that his face cannot go under the water's surface.

At this age, most babies like to jump up and down in water, although they are also likely to play happily just sitting or standing. Your child will probably dislike getting splashed or having water in his face. One of the best ways for him to see how to play in the water is for you to let him splash you and see you enjoying the water, too. Before you put his feet in, make sure yours are wet. He'll follow your lead.

Playgrounds

Slides, space to run, swings—playgrounds are a child's idea of heaven. As a parent, you will learn to love them, too. For one thing, while you'll still have to watch your child, she will most likely be off and running to have a good time and you will be able to use your eyes more than your hands.

Nevertheless, a playground is not designed with a one-year-old in mind, so you have to be very mindful of her safety. If possible, find structures that are for smaller children (some are labeled as toddler areas), and always have your hand nearby so she can catch it. She is not old enough to hold onto anything herself, and it is likely that she doesn't yet realize that if she lets go she can fall.

At the age of one, your child will enjoy the baby swing (she needs to be strapped in or in a harness), climbing up the steps of the structures older kids climb and race on, sitting on rocking-horse type structures, and maybe sitting on a see-saw while you hold her and move her up and down.

 Essential

> Unless it is specifically designed for toddlers, most playground equipment will be difficult for your one-year-old to negotiate. You may need to get involved with her—sit on the swing and hold her on it, get on the slide and go down with her. Show her how it's done and how much fun it is!

Slides and monkey bars used to have concrete at the base. These days, most playgrounds use sawdust or wood chips to soften landings. Nevertheless, you'll need to stay close. Slips and falls happen quickly, and a one-year-old is less steady on these types of surfaces than an older child would be.

Your child will like watching other children, too, so make sure you keep her far from where kids are swinging and where crowds of children are running.

One-year-olds love open space, and the freedom of a playground will give them a lot to explore. They may not want to leave, so get ready to stay awhile! When you do intend to leave, give your child plenty of warning. Let her know when you'll be leaving and what activity is planned next, even if it's just the drive home. Moving from one activity to the next is hard for one-year-olds. Your child may cry or get angry. The less attention you pay to this behavior, and the more you focus on the fun she had, the more likely she is to calm down.

Chapter 8

Nutrition

A one-year-old doesn't know about nutrition or calories. A one-year-old thinks food is no different from anything else around him—a joyful science experiment just waiting to be played with in every way possible. Therefore, while he's busy having fun with his meals, you'll probably be trying to make sure his food is nutritious and that he's eating enough. If that sounds like a struggle just waiting to happen, rest assured that most one-year-olds eat plenty even though they mash their food, pile it, and move it around the plate.

Feeding Your One-Year-Old

Many pediatricians recommend that mothers breastfeed for the first year. After that, it is up to a mother and child to determine whether breastfeeding should continue. Weaning is the process of helping your child make the transition from breastfeeding or bottle-feeding (which can include feedings of breast milk, cow's milk, or soy milk) to solid food.

As a one-year-old, your baby may already be weaned, but it is also possible that you are still breastfeeding or bottle-feeding exclusively, are just beginning to prepare for the weaning process, or have started to feed a combination of breast milk and solid foods. Many moms, at this point, are only breastfeeding at night, a time when she can cuddle quietly with her baby and when the time together and the act of sucking may make falling asleep easier for her baby.

Giving up the breast or bottle is a big step for your baby, but it's a struggle for parents as well. It means their child is no longer a baby and doesn't need them in quite the same way as she used to.

This time is especially charged with emotion for mothers who have been breastfeeding to this point. Nursing a child is an emotional connection just as much as a physical one. This is one of the first times you'll be "letting go" of a common experience with your child. As your hormones shift and change, you may find the experience especially poignant. It might be helpful to discuss your feelings with a friend or your partner. Just being open and honest about your feelings will take off some pressure. Talking to moms of babies who are weaning is also a great source of support.

When to Wean

You'll hear a lot of different advice, some of it conflicting, on the subject of when is the right time to wean your child. After the age of six months, your child's digestive system is developed enough to handle solid foods. He may, however, still demonstrate the "tongue thrust" reflex, in which the tongue automatically pushes solids out of the mouth. Babies can be expected to dribble and drool. But if the tongue thrust happens consistently, it is a sign that your baby is not ready for solids. Wait a few weeks before you try again. Here are a few other developmental milestones that most experts agree he should meet before he's ready to begin eating:

- The ability to pick up small objects with the "pincer" grasp (between thumb and forefinger) rather than the "palmar" grasp, in which the baby uses fingers to sweep an object into his palm and pick it up that way
- The ability to sit up without assistance
- The ability to detect satiation; that is, to stop eating when full (instead of always falling asleep at the end of the meal, as very young babies do)

Some experts also counsel that it's time to wean when your child begins paying eager attention to the food you're eating. Some babies begin reaching for their parents' plates very early, apparently attracted by the smell and appearance of grownup food. While your baby is very likely to find your food interesting, it is hard to know whether that interest truly does comes from the desire to eat. At one year of age, most babies are attracted to any object their parents are holding—

and most babies are eager to put anything into their mouths, edible or not.

 Alert!

> If your child is in day care, her caregivers may insist that she give up her bottle during the day once she's walking steadily. If this is the case, let this help lead your child into a new stage of development, using a cup to drink from and objects other than a bottle (such as a stuffed animal) for comfort.

Your child's behavior is another way to tell whether it's time to begin weaning. You may find that he's hungry more often, and that a nursing session no longer satisfies him for as long as it used to. Babies do go through growth spurts during which they are naturally hungrier than usual, and since breast milk is metabolized very quickly, it's also natural for a breast-feeding baby to be frequently hungry. As he becomes more interested in the sight and smell of food, however, you might want to take the opportunity to begin introducing solids.

How to Wean

As you have probably already discovered if you've begun researching this topic, different people swear by many different approaches to weaning. Some people counsel against introducing fruits before vegetables or meats, saying that fruit is so sweet that your baby will never want anything else. (Actually, hardly any food is sweeter than breast milk—don't worry that your baby will become addicted to bananas or fructose in any other form.) Others warn against feeding foods of certain colors, saying that orange foods like sweet potatoes and squash are only safe for older babies.

There are only two real things to worry about in weaning. First, you want to be sure your baby can swallow the solids you feed her without choking. Second, you want to be sure you are feeding foods she can safely digest and that are unlikely to cause an allergic reaction.

Most people begin feeding rice cereal and then move to fruits, vegetables, and meats, in that order. You could just as easily start with a soft palatable fruit, like banana or avocado. Introduce only one food at a time—if you start with cereal, feed only that for four days. If your baby is allergic, she will have a reaction within that time, and you will know exactly what caused it. After the four days are up, you can introduce a new food. Continue like this until you have a repertoire of foods you are sure you can feed safely. At that point, you can begin to mix foods—peas and carrots are a popular combination, or puréed chicken and squash.

The goal in weaning is to introduce your child to the taste and texture of solid food. This can be a long process. Don't despair in the first few feedings if most of the food goes on, rather than in, your baby. The concept of food as something that can be looked at and touched is brand new to your child. She needs time to familiarize herself with the idea. It can take a dozen times for a baby to accept a new food, so if your baby doesn't seem to like anything you feed her, don't give up.

Sometimes the texture of a food will surprise your baby, making her gag or look surprised. Keep smiling even if she's making a funny face and give her a moment to get used to the flavor or texture of a food. Let your child play with her food so that she doesn't feel pressure to either like it or dislike it. She's going to have her own individual taste and preferences, right from the beginning.

Weaning Step by Step

Eventually your child will actually be eating solid foods, instead of wearing them, and will no longer rely on milk for her sustenance. At that point, the most common approach to weaning is to slowly phase out your daily liquid feeding sessions. Drop one a week until the only liquid feeding time is at night, before bed. Begin by cutting back on the times when your baby shows the least interest in the breast or bottle, such as in the morning or after lunch.

Frequently, the last time to wean is at bedtime. To do this, give your baby breastfeeding or bottle-feeding time before your actual bedtime routine so that she begins to learn other comforting routines (such as listening to a story or having his back rubbed) rather than relying on your breast to go to sleep. If bedtime becomes difficult in the end stages of weaning, you may need to have your partner put your child to bed for a few weeks until the nighttime feeding experience has been forgotten by your baby (and it will be). This substitute transition may make the experience less stressful for both mom and baby.

Whole Food

Your baby is probably eating in a high chair or booster seat at the table and possibly finds the foods you and other adults eat fascinating. During this year, your child will be able to alternate between whole foods (cut into small pieces) and baby food, which is typically puréed.

As long as the foods you give your baby are natural with little additional fat and sugar, then it's your preference (and his) as to what form of food he eats. Puréed food is better if he has very few teeth or needs to be fed with a spoon, but as he gets a little older, he'll be fine with small pieces of food that he can pick up and feed to himself.

 Essential

Even if your baby prefers a bottle, she is capable of holding and drinking from a cup with handles or a sippy cup (the type that doesn't spill when knocked over). Sippy cups allow her to suck liquid up, which is safer than a regular cup because she won't get too much liquid in her mouth at once.

When preparing whole food for your child, you'll need to be sure it is easy for him to chew and digest, as well as handle with his fingers. Peel fruits, since apple skins, for example, are difficult for little tongues to handle. Likewise, peel vegetables, such as carrots. You should also steam or boil carrots and other vegetables to make them softer for your child. Meats are often difficult for young children to chew and swallow, so making these into purées is the best idea.

A good snack—like a healthy meal—is composed of a protein (egg, cheese, meat) and a carbohydrate (fruit, vegetables, whole-grain bread) as well as a little natural fat (such as that found in the protein foods). Most snacks that are convenient, such as chips and sugary foods, are not nutritious and won't help your child feel full. They may also contribute to bad moods and irritability.

Baby Food

Many one-year-olds are ready to move from jarred baby foods, which are very soft, to finger foods, which are also packaged by food manufacturers. These products are often just the right size for little fingers, and the noodles and little bits of chicken or beef are small enough for them to swallow without choking.

When purchasing baby food, look for all-natural and organic products with little or no added fat and sugar. Read the ingredient list to see if sugar, for example, has been added to tomato sauce or a lot of salt has been put into an entrée. Your child does not need a lot of added seasonings to be stimulated and attracted to his food. The only place where he might need some flavor is with his vegetables, since the bitterness of broccoli, for example, can offend a young child's palate. However, you can purchase puréed vegetable combinations (such as broccoli and carrots) that are naturally sweeter without added fat or sugar.

Portion Sizes

Your child's stomach is very small, only slightly larger than your fist, so she can't fit a lot of food into it at once. Parents often think their child isn't eating enough, even if she acts full or stops eating, but really, children are naturally good judges of how much they should eat. She will want to graze throughout the day, and you should offer her frequent snacks so that her mood and energy level stay relatively even. At any one time, your one-year-old will only need about the amount of food that fits into a small child-sized bowl (one- to three-quarters of a cup). A quarter cup of noodles, one slice of turkey, slices of a small apple, or a few orange sections are enough for one sitting.

Choking Hazards

A one-year-old must always be watched when he's eating because he can easily choke if he puts too much food in his mouth. Most small children have a habit of stuffing their mouths full. Encourage your child to take very small bites and to chew. Some foods that a one-year-old should not be given are nuts, whole grapes, large pieces of meat, unpeeled fruits and vegetables, and popcorn.

If you notice your child gagging, move his head forward and put your finger in his mouth and try to get the food out without moving your finger near his throat. If your baby doesn't seem to be breathing or if he begins to get very red, he may truly be choking. Call 911 immediately.

Milk

At the age of one, your child can begin to drink cow's milk. (She shouldn't have it until then because her stomach can't easily digest the protein.) Children should always drink whole milk, as the fat is vital for brain development. This shouldn't replace breast milk (if you're still breastfeeding) but should instead be considered a serving from the dairy food group, as are cheese and yogurt. Your child should have about 200 calories of calcium-rich foods a day, which equals a glass of milk, a slice of cheese, and a small serving of yogurt.

Dairy products are great snacks for children, since they are often portable and easy to divide into single servings. Some dairy is even sold in single servings, such as string cheese and yogurt. Dairy foods are just as important as, and in some ways healthier than, other foods for toddlers. Yogurts and cheeses are especially good ways for children to get calcium, protein, and other nutrients. At this age, snacking is an opportunity for your child to get important nutrition breaks, since her stomach can't hold a large meal.

 Alert!

Chocolate milk is not necessarily bad for children, but it does have a lot of added sugar—it's not just chocolate that makes the flavor so appealing. Consider it a treat for your baby and not a regular part of her diet.

Lactose Intolerance

Some children don't tolerate the sugars and proteins in milk well and get stomachaches after drinking milk. If people in your family are lactose intolerant, keep an eye on your child, as she will be more likely to have this problem. Smelly, loose stools are a sign of this digestion problem. If you suspect your child is lactose intolerant, talk to your pediatrician. He may be able to recommend an over-the-counter medicine that will help your child better digest milk products; or he may need to drink other types of milk, such as soy. The good news about lactose intolerance is that many children can eat other dairy foods, such as hard cheeses and yogurts, even if their digestive systems can't handle straight milk.

Hormones in Milk

Most diary cows today are fed a large number of hormones to increase milk production. These hormones—which are typically estrogen or female hormone variations—stay in the milk, which is then consumed by humans. More and more research is showing that these hormones may have a detrimental effect on children (both boys and girls) as they grow up, and may even cause the early onset puberty of and other hormonal changes. Look for milk and other food products that are made without hormones (it usually says so on the label).

Food Jags

When a one-year-old finds a food he likes, he will often seem obsessed with it, only wanting to eat macaroni and cheese, for example, or endlessly munching on cantaloupe. Part of your child's food obsession is happiness. He has discovered something he likes, a flavor or texture, and wants to continue enjoying it. Chances are that if you let him follow through with this and, at the same time, put new foods as well as favorites on his plate, he will eventually return to eating a variety. However, if you point any of this out to him, you'll set up a struggle. Instead, let him follow his own urges and desires, which will naturally bring him to want a variety of foods.

Keep the variety coming, whether your child eats what you offer or not, so that he may branch out and at least try something other than his favorites. Variety is a key part of good nutrition. During this year, your child will not be eating as voraciously as he once did (since he's not growing as much), but he will eat enough to keep growing.

Your child's food likes and dislikes do not predict what he will be like as an adult eater, but the way you teach him to relate to food can help determine whether he will have a healthy attitude toward food as he grows up. Will he eat mostly for energy and health, or will he want to eat lots of junk? Will he be able to listen to his appetite in order to maintain a healthy weight, or will he overeat and gain weight?

Try to dismiss the attitude that you have to get your child to eat. Instead, help him learn to listen to his body and eat foods that will keep him healthy and happy. To do this, ask him if he's hungry or full so that he tries to decipher the meanings of those words and how they relate to the feelings in his body. Always offer healthy foods and encourage limited treats. Explain why the foods you are giving him are nutritious and healthy. Saying, "Carrots help you see better!" or "Noodles give you energy!" may not make for the most scintillating conversation, but communicating the connection between food and the way your baby's body works will start a lifelong healthy relationship with eating.

Detecting Food Allergies

These days, food allergies are a hot topic. Whether it's peanuts, milk, or soy, many parents are told that they cannot bring certain foods into day care because of a child with an allergy. According to the National Allergy and Infectious Diseases, a division of the U.S. Department of Health and Human Services, about 150 Americans, mostly adults and adolescents, die of food allergies each year. In fact, most "allergies" are actually intolerances, which means the body can't digest a certain food, such as milk, and an upset stomach occurs. True food allergies are extremely rare and only affect 6 to 8 percent of children, and only 4 percent of those kids still have the allergies as adults. Meanwhile, peanut and tree nut allergies (the allergies most parents hear about, as they cause the most severe food-induced allergic reactions) affect approximately 0.6 percent and 0.4 percent of Americans respectively.

 Fact

When a person is allergic to something, whether it's a food or a substance such as pollen or cat dander, the immune system goes into overdrive when that person is near the allergen or if she happens to eat it. As a result, the skin or respiratory system reacts with hives, skin irritation, or breathing problems.

A food allergy is an extreme reaction and happens quickly. If a child is allergic to strawberries, for example, you will very quickly see hives, or she may tell you that she has trouble breathing. If this happens, immediately bring your child to a doctor or emergency room, as the allergic reaction can become more severe very quickly. You can try giving your child Benadryl or another over-the-counter anti-allergy remedy, but call the doctor first. Be sure to seek medical care if your child develops any swelling in her face or neck or has trouble breathing.

Genetic Predisposition

Allergies tend to run in families, so if you, your partner, or people in your family suffer from allergies, you should be on the lookout for allergies in your children. The first allergic reaction is often mild, so take it seriously and discuss it with a pediatrician, because the next exposure, whether to a food or a substance, could cause a more severe reaction.

Common Allergens

The most common food allergens are:

- Strawberries
- Milk
- Wheat
- Shellfish
- Soy
- Chocolate
- Nuts
- Eggs

Usually if a parent or close relative has an allergy to one of these foods, a child will be predisposed to having the allergy.

Some children are allergic to additives, such as monosodium glutamate (MSG), which is a flavor enhancer found in many canned and some restaurant foods, most notably

Chinese food. If you notice that your child undergoes a behavioral change after eating certain foods, try turning to whole foods, such as fruits, vegetables, whole grains, fish, meat, and poultry—anything that is farmed or hunted and hasn't been highly processed—to take the additives out of your child's diet. This is a purer diet (especially if you choose organic foods) and one that is less likely to cause problems.

Many children grow out of their allergies, or their allergic reactions change as they get older. The most important thing is that you need to listen to your own experience of your child's eating and behavior interactions. At this age, it is easy to take a food out of his diet if it seems to cause a problem.

However, because an allergic reaction can be dangerous, it's important to tell anyone who cares for your child about the sensitivity. If your child has a severe reaction, including difficulty breathing, then everyone must be made aware of what your child is allergic to and be sure he isn't exposed to the irritant. The signs of a severe reaction include dizziness, difficulty breathing, sweating, and the possibility of passing out.

Hives, a skin reaction with raised red bumps, is a common allergic reaction to both foods and contact irritants, such as laundry detergents. To deal with them, use a hydrocortisone or anti-itch cream and try to determine what caused the reaction in order to cut the food or other irritant (such as fragranced soap) out of your child's daily routine.

Fruit and Juice

Fruit is an important part of your child's diet, as it provides a lot of vitamins and minerals without a lot of calories or fat.

The sugar in fruit is a good source of energy, and fruit is also often loaded with antioxidants, which are important for good health.

Lots of parents turn to fruit juice instead of real fruit because it saves them time peeling and slicing fresh fruit. Fruit juice has some benefits but also its share of problems. The benefit of juice is that it is comparable to fresh fruit in terms of the nutrients it provides. Also, it is sometimes easier for a child to drink juice than it is to eat fruit. Unfortunately, many of the juices that are packaged specifically for children have a high amount of added sugar, which a real fruit juice does not need to be flavorful. Also, fruit juice blends are sometimes composed mostly of apple or white grape juice, both of which are less nutrient-rich than cranberry, purple grape, or citrus fruit drinks (such as orange, mango, or papaya). Juice also lacks the fiber found in fresh fruit, and thus does not leave your child feeling full or as satisfied.

 **Alert!**

When buying juice, look for varieties without pulp or those that are the least pulpy. Pulp can get stuck in a cup, as well as in a child's throat and teeth. Also, you can always add water to your child's juice to decrease the amount of calories she is drinking.

You should always read the labels of the juice drinks you buy. If the label lists any added sugars, or if the first ingredients are white grape juice or apple juice, look for another brand.

Dietary Guidelines

Toddlers need to eat enough calories from all the food groups to stay energetic, be happy, and yet stay within their weight guidelines. As your child begins to walk and become more physically active, she will need more calories, but she won't gain much weight. Instead, her body will thin out and grow longer. Nevertheless, she will need to have a steady stream of food to keep moving so much.

 Fact

> Processed foods, which often have added chemicals and sugars, are often high in calories and fat but low in nutrients. They aren't filling because they aren't nutritious, and yet they can easily make anyone, including children, gain weight. Try to reduce the amount of processed foods your children eat, which will help them stay healthy and at the proper weight.

Your child's biggest food sources should be cereals, fruit, and vegetables. The next group should be protein, with dairy foods close behind. Fats should be the smallest type of food she eats, and added sugar should not be in her daily diet at all. The natural sugars found in fruits, some vegetables, and dairy foods are healthy and should not be cut out of her diet.

Like adults, toddlers need to eat balanced meals. Balanced meals are those that contain correct proportions of major food groups. These include carbohydrates (fruits, vegetables, whole grains), proteins (meats, fish, poultry, and legumes), and fats (oils, animal products). Your child does not need added salt or sugary foods in her diet. She can eat whole-fat foods, such as milk, cottage cheese, or yogurt, but she does not need a lot of added butter or oil in her meals. She should drink water, milk, or real fruit juice with her meals.

Many parents mistakenly believe their children will only eat what are now considered to be childhood staples—hot dogs, chicken nuggets, and macaroni and cheese. But the truth is that, to some extent, parents control what their children eat. While you can't control how much your child eats, you do control what types of food she eats. If you offer fish rather than hot dogs, baked chicken rather than fried, or whole-wheat noodles rather than macaroni and cheese, your child will eat those foods. And even if she refuses them at first, once she gets hungry, she'll eat what's in front of her.

Chapter 9

Safety and First Aid

The main safety challenges for one-year-olds stem from their ability to move and their curiosity. During this year, your child's mobility will make it easier for him to reach and touch more objects than he used to. His increased speed and feelings of confidence make accidents more likely to occur than they were when he was being carried around. The good new is that accidents, especially serious ones, are often preventable. If you take appropriate precautions, you will ensure that your one-year-old will be able to happily and safely explore his world.

Car Seat Basics

A one-year-old child has developed enough muscular strength and coordination to sit in a forward-facing car seat, though the seat must still be installed in the back seat of your car. Even though you've kept your child in the back seat for at least a year now, you might not know why it's important for him to ride there. There are two reasons. First, the point of impact in most car accidents is in the front, so your child is safer in the back. Second, the back seat has no air bags. Air bags are dangerous for children because they are designed for adults. The force with which the air bags deploy can severely injure a child. Children are safest in the middle of the back seat. All back doors should be locked, and windows should be closed using the child safety lock feature.

Car Seat Options

All car seats sold in reputable stores have passed federal safety standards, and most cost somewhere around $100. A cost above that is usually for the material or design elements, as it is not necessarily true that a more expensive seat is safer. You can also buy a car seat that turns into a booster seat when your child weighs more and is taller. These are just as safe as other car seats—especially if they have a five-point harness. Always head to the police or fire station to have an expert check that the seat is installed properly.

Your driving will be safer if your baby isn't fussy, so it's important to make sure his ride is set up in a way that's entertaining as well as safe. At one year of age, your baby is facing forward and watching you drive. He might enjoy having a pretend steering wheel to play with, as well as toys near his seat, but don't add anything to the seat that might get in the way of the straps or handles. Other dangers include anything that could go flying in a crash.

Proper Strapping

A properly installed and strapped car seat reduces the chance of a fatal injury by 54 percent in children ages one to four, according to the National Highway Traffic Safety Administration (✍*www.nhtsa.gov*). An unrestrained child sitting in a car that crashes at just twenty-five miles per hour is subject to the same impact as being dropped out of a third-floor window. And a child who is simply held in an adult's lap and not restrained in a car seat at all will take only one-tenth of a second to hit the dashboard—and that's also at the same low speed.

 Fact

A five-point harness—the strapping system that wraps across your child's chest as well as his lap—is effective because it keeps your baby from receiving the force of impact in any one part of his body during an accident. The harness spreads out the impact and keeps your child in the seat.

The car seat must be tight against the car's seat itself and, if necessary, the belt that holds the car seat in might need a hook or special lock to keep the seat steady and flush against the car. The chest clip that is part of all car seats should be level with your child's armpit, while the lap belt should be across her hips.

Finally, be sure your child isn't bulked up by coats and blankets underneath the belts and straps. If it's cold, be sure the straps are flush against his clothes (so that he is secured in the seat) and then cover him with a blanket to keep him warm.

Be aware that car seats have an expiration date. Do not use a car seat past the date printed on the seat. Also, if the seat has been in an accident, it is no longer safe to use, according to national safety standards. You may not need to replace the car seat if you were in a very minor accident. The National Highway Traffic Safety Administration defines a minor accident as one that meets all of the following criteria:

- The vehicle was able to be driven away from the crash site.
- The vehicle door nearest the safety seat was undamaged.
- There were no injuries to any of the vehicle occupants.
- The air bags (if present) did not deploy.
- There is no visible damage to the safety seat.

If you were in a very minor accident, get your car seat inspected at a child seat inspection station. To find one near you, go online to the National Highway Traffic Safety Administration Web site, at ✐*www.nhtsa.gov.*

Childproofing the House

Now that your child is roaming freely throughout the house, you're going to have to think like a one-year-old to anticipate her moves and be sure she will be safe. A one-year-old, of course, doesn't think so much as explore and experiment. She will go everywhere and touch everything, and much of the going and the touching will take place with all of her fingers, her entire body, and her mouth.

Watch your child closely for a few days and notice where she goes when she's exploring. Move anything toxic (such as cleansers, lotions, and food) out of her reach and then lock the cabinet where those things are stored. Use childproof locks to secure the toilet as well as any cabinets and doors that she can open. Be sure any weapons in the house are not loaded and are in a locked cabinet with the bullets or accessories kept in a separate place. Childproofing is a process that will take place over a few days because you'll keep noticing new places your child can explore. Also, those places will change over the coming year as your one-year-old gets bigger and stronger.

One of the most important places you'll want to keep your child from exploring on her own is the staircase. Because she is just learning to walk, she will be very interested in going up and down the stairs. While it's fine for her to practice when you're nearby, steps and an unsteady toddler are not a good match. Childproof your stairs by placing baby gates at the top and the bottom.

While many toddlers like to walk up stairs (very slowly), they mostly practice some form of sliding or climbing down them. It is often safer for your one-year-old to bump down the steps or to turn around and slide on her belly than it is for her to walk down, which requires depth perception and balance skills that she may not yet have mastered. If your child doesn't try these methods on her own, you might want to teach her and encourage her to slide, rather than walk, down the stairs in your house.

Electrical Outlets and Equipment

Many parents know they should get child safety plugs to be sure their children don't put their fingers, or anything else, into electrical outlets. Outlets, however, are just the beginning. Wires and appliances should all be carefully taped down or hidden from your toddlers. Children can get electrical burns and can be electrocuted from chewing on wires.

While few toddlers get hurt by electronic equipment such as VCRs or DVD players, children can easily break them if they touch the buttons repeatedly or try to move them in order to study them more closely. Keep anything you don't want your child to play with out of his sight and reach.

Heavy TVs and stereos can fall—more easily than you think—on a small, curious child who tries to touch their buttons and pull on their wires. Even dressers and bureaus can fall on your child, especially if he tries to open the drawers and climb on them. If anything in your house is loose or easy to pull, protect your child and secure that item using locks, bolts, or chains. Things to consider securing include TVs, stereos, desktop computers, and heavy furniture.

Corners and Edges

As one-year-olds learn to walk and explore the world around them, they will inevitably fall and will often take a bump on the head (or knee or elbow), on the way down. Likewise, as they cruise along holding onto furniture, they will grab onto whatever is nearby. Covering up corners and edges will ensure that your child's bumps are not serious.

You can find edge and corner covers—which stick to furniture with adhesive—at stores that sell baby goods and at some large hardware stores. You should take care to cover fireplace edges and the edges of radiators, especially if they are on the floor and made of metal—these can be sharp enough to leave a pretty nasty gash on a one-year-old's head! Gates should be put around fireplaces, radiators, and wood stoves, too, so that a baby won't walk over and touch them.

Cabinets

A cabinet is like a mystery box to a small child. The under-sink cabinets in the bathroom and kitchen, as well as those in wall installments, are on the same level as a one-year-old, and unless you install special latches they will be easy for your child to open. One-year-olds will want to open cabinets, take everything out, play with and possibly eat it, and perhaps climb inside the cabinet. Cabinet locks and guards are especially important safety devices. They should always be kept on cabinets that hold medicine, cleaning supplies, tools, and anything that a child might want to taste, such as food, soap, perfume, and liquids.

 Essential

If your child is endlessly curious about cabinets, you might give her one filled with toys and things she can play with, such as pots and pans, plastic containers, and toys.

Accidents Happen

Even with all of the safety precautions you think to take, your child will bump her head, open cabinets and take something out that she shouldn't, and walk into the edges of doors. Amazingly, most of her injuries will be minor. When she does get hurt, don't ignore her pain and fear. Acknowledge that it hurts and reassure her. Make sure she doesn't have a cut that needs a bandage or other medical care, and then help her get past the injury. Give her something else to play with, or take her to a different room. If she still seems upset or frightened, show her how to correctly perform that action that resulted in her injury so that she feels more confident and safe.

Children respond very positively when adults acknowledge and validate their experiences. At the same time, they need to hear your opinion about what happened because they trust that the adult more fully understands the situation. So, if you say, "Oh, that must have hurt. I never like it when I fall and bump my head. But I see that you're okay, so maybe we can do something else now," it takes care of their feelings and allows them to rely on you for reassurance.

Staying Safe Outside

Communicating safety issues to a child is a delicate balancing act. Part of a parent's responsibility is to not be too obsessed with safety. Don't make your child feel that you don't trust his abilities. You want your child to feel safe and be safe without making him worried or scared that he will get hurt easily. Explain safety issues to your child without putting the focus on his abilities. For example, rather than saying, "I think you're going to fall," you might say, "Do you see how these steps are uneven? They are hard to walk on." A one-year-old has no idea that much of what fascinates him outside, from cars to animals to nature, can be dangerous. And while no one wants to discourage a child from the outdoors, this is an age when you really have to keep a close eye on your child.

 Alert!

If you have a sandbox in your back yard, be sure to keep it covered at night or when you're not using it. Animals may use that area as a pit stop, and you don't want your child getting in there before you check it for droppings.

One good idea for keeping your young child safe outdoors is to have an area that he can play in, but one that isn't so big that you have to continually chase him or stand nearby. If you have a very large back yard, consider fencing off an area. It will be a good way to keep all his outdoor toys together and to keep him contained so that he can't get near a pool or hot tub or other dangerous areas that might hold lawn equipment or tools.

Moving Vehicles

One-year-olds can move very quickly when they want to and are able to zip from the back yard to the driveway, for instance, or to run off in a busy parking lot. They can get into the garage before you know it, too. While many parents spend a lot of energy making sure their young children are buckled into their car seats properly, it's also important that parents and other adults be very aware of children when they are outside of the car. If you are planning to drive anywhere when you know your child is playing outside, check your mirrors carefully. If you know your child is close by but can't see her in your mirrors, get out of the car and look around to be sure she is safe before you drive off.

Steps and Balconies

Outdoor steps are often difficult for children to navigate, as they can be made from slate, brick, or other uneven materials, and they don't always have railings. Because one-year-olds don't yet have a great sense of balance and their legs are not always able to negotiate the space from one step to another easily, it is much more difficult for them to step down than it is for them to climb up. Always offer your hand to your child when he's approaching stairs. You may have to carry your child upstairs until he is two.

Balconies usually have bars and railings, but children can easily slip through these. A child should never be on a balcony alone, as he will want to climb and explore past the protected boundaries.

Pool Safety

Foam bubbles, water wings, life jackets, and other certified flotation devices are a must for a baby near water. Even if you are holding your child, she should always have something on her body that will keep her afloat if something should happen while she's in or near the water. While your child may be able to naturally paddle or seems to be able to stay afloat in the water, she should never be considered a swimmer. Pools should have fences and covers, as well as motion detectors and sensors so that small children do not get into them when no one is looking. These sensors are available at hardware stores, pool supply stores, and Web sites and stores that sell child-safety equipment, such as *www.childsafetystore.com.*

 Essential

> If you are going to an outdoor party, ask if there is a pool. Always bring a flotation device for your child. If you have neighbors with pools, work with them on making sure they are fenced properly. For above-ground pool safety, the ladder should be pulled up if no adult is around.

Many one-year-olds love playing in kiddie pools, which are those small plastic pools you can buy at most pool and toy stores and that you fill with water from a garden hose. Do not leave your child alone near a kiddie pool, and put water wings on her if she wants to try to swim or float. Always empty the pool after you're done using it. That way your child can't somehow wander to it and fall in while you are distracted, and you won't be leaving the water in the pool to get dirty. Kiddie pool water doesn't have chlorine in it to kill germs.

Choking Prevention

You have probably already noticed how many toys carry tags and labels saying "Not suitable for children under 3." There is good reason for those warnings. Young children very quickly put things in their mouths and then accidentally swallow them. Money, parts of toys, and small foods can all be choking hazards for a one-year-old.

If you see your child's hand closed in a fist, always check that he isn't clutching something small in it. If you notice that he's holding his mouth closed, be sure he isn't hiding something in there. If your child does get something in his mouth, try to get him to spit it out rather than putting your fingers in his mouth or throat, which can push the item farther down. If your child doesn't spit anything out, tilt his head forward and swipe your finger in his mouth without reaching in too deeply. A rule to keep in mind is that one-year-olds cannot be trusted with anything that is smaller than their thumbs.

In addition to putting things in their mouths, one-year-olds also love to stick things up their noses. If something gets stuck in your child's nostril, do not try to take it out yourself. Instead, take him to the doctor or emergency room.

Balloons aren't small, but they do break, and pieces of balloon are the number-one cause of asphyxiation in small children. According to the *Journal of the American Medical Association,* nearly one-third of children who choke to death each year (most of whom were eight or younger) do so on latex balloons. Your child can easily put a balloon fragment into her mouth quickly. Because balloon material is slippery, it gets caught easily in the windpipe.

While children love balloons and they are everywhere children are, they are dangerous. Being aware of their danger is a good first step in preventing a choking problem, but you can take other levels of prevention. First, if a balloon breaks, double- and triple-check that all of the pieces have been found and thrown away. Second, do not let a small child put her mouth near a balloon (which she will want to do). Third, and most importantly, don't buy balloons.

The strings of balloons, as well as the strings on other toys, are also a potential problem for children, as they can wrap them around their wrists and necks. Simply being aware of the ways in which a one-year-old can misuse things like string is your best defense against a problem. A one-year-old should only play with string under your supervision.

Learning CPR

If your child's breathing has stopped—for whatever reason— it is imperative that you do all you can to get it started again. Do not leave the child. Have another adult call 911. If the child isn't alert, shake him to try to get him to wake up.

 Alert!

Parents should take a first-aid and CPR course to deal with accidents that might happen to their children, as well as children who will visit their house. To learn more, call your local YMCA or Red Cross. See Appendix A for more resource information.

Then, remember the ABCs of resuscitation:

- **Airway:** Put the child on his back, tilt his chin up, open his mouth, and sweep your fingers through his mouth to take anything out that may be obstructing his airway.

- **Breathing:** If your child isn't breathing, you must breathe for him until help arrives.
- **Circulation:** Check for a pulse. If he doesn't have a pulse, you'll have to use CPR to get his heart pumping again.

Nothing replaces a CPR certification course when it comes to the knowledge and experience needed to practice CPR, so while the following instructions give you the basics, you should know that in a class, you will practice on a dummy and do it in real-time. This practice will make your actions second nature and correct. Here are the basic steps to performing CPR:

1. Lie your child down on his back, tilt his chin up, and inhale. Then, place your entire mouth over his mouth and nostrils and exhale deeply and slowly to get air into his body.
2. Remove your lips and check for a pulse again. If there is no pulse, put your fingers in the middle of his chest, below his nipples, and press down five times, counting to two between presses. Then breathe again into your baby's mouth.
3. Keep doing this until he begins to breathe again or until help arrives.

All parents should take a class in child safety. There is no substitute for learning this technique in person from a certified teacher. Always be sure your child's teachers, babysitters, and any close relatives are also knowledgeable about CPR for children.

Cuts and Bruises

Cuts and bruises are the most common injuries you will have to deal with as a parent. For the most part, your role will be to wipe away tears, offer a hug, and explain what happened ("You tripped on the toy, so let's put it away" or "You need to be careful when you're close to the table"). This will help your child pay attention to her surroundings, while also helping her see that she can recover from a small injury.

Every home should have a complete first-aid kit, and a home with a one-year-old should also have adhesive bandages of every size and shape as well as gauze and tape. Most adhesive bandages are not designed with a small body in mind, and you will sometimes have to be creative when it comes to finding the right one to cover a cut or to stay on a body that wriggles a lot and gets wet and dirty easily.

 Essential

Fun adhesive bandages, covered with cartoon characters and other designs, help children stop focusing on their cuts. Even though they serve no extra medicinal purpose, the designs are a good way to make a child's boo-boos a little less frightening.

A scrape is the most superficial type of cut. With a scrape, the first couple of layers of skin are removed but the cut doesn't go down below the skin. Scrapes can hurt, though, so your child may feel better with an adhesive bandage. You should rinse the scrape with cool water to clean the wound and alleviate some of the throbbing pain that accompanies a scrape. Make sure to get any gravel or sand out of the wound, and then cover with antiseptic cream and a bandage.

A cut is deeper than a scrape. Cuts are generally narrow incisions that tend to bleed. Most cuts also just require a little antiseptic (such as hydrogen peroxide or antiseptic cream) and an adhesive bandage, but if the cut is bleeding a lot, you should clean the wound and consider whether it requires stitches. You should see a doctor about stitches if a child's cut is deeper than a quarter-inch or if it gapes open (meaning that it opens like a fish's mouth).

It's scary for a child to see his own blood (and to his parent, as well). If your child does get a bad cut, it's one of those moments when you'll really have to be a grown-up and not let your child see any reaction other than calm capability. If you can, raise the injured area of the body to help slow the flow of blood. The body part should be elevated at least a few inches, but not so much that your child is uncomfortable. Cover the wound with something clean and absorbent and apply gentle pressure to the wound. This will help stop the bleeding and will also hide the wound, which might help calm your child.

If your child gets hysterical or overly upset about the bleeding, try to have someone else talk to him or soothe him while you clean and bandage his cut. If this is impossible, keep talking to him while you fix him up.

A cut on a baby's head can look scary because scalp wounds can bleed a lot even when they aren't necessarily deeper or more serious than other cuts. However, you should always be extra-cautious with head cuts and bumps because of the danger of internal injury, such as concussion.

 Alert!

> If your child's accident results in clear fluid or blood leaking from his ears or nose, immediately bring him to a doctor or emergency room. This can indicate a skull injury. Also be on the lookout for any behavioral changes, such as lethargy or fatigue.

If your child seems to lose consciousness, is drowsy or nauseated, or has trouble hearing or responding to you within twenty-four hours of hitting his head, bring him to the doctor or an emergency room right away. If his head is swelling, put some ice on it and keep an eye on him. The swelling should go down, not get worse, and while it's natural for bruises to change color, they should not get bloody or fill with fluid.

Insect Bites

The most important thing you need to know about insect bites and young children is that you won't detect an allergy, if one exists, until your child has been bitten. You'll need to be aware of the potential for that problem if you see an insect bite—which usually looks like a small red bump—on your child's skin.

If your child is stung on soft tissue—such as in his mouth, around his genitals, or near his eye—bring him to a doctor.

A sting in a one-year-old's mouth can obstruct his breathing and, a sting on or near the eye should be looked at by a professional, in case any part of the eyeball is injured.

Bee Stings

Bee stings hurt and surprise young children. One-year-olds are often terrified of bees and wasps because they understand early on that these insects sting. If a bee or wasp is flying around your child, teach your child to sit still. This will discourage the bee from feeling threatened and stinging.

Very few people are truly allergic to bees. Most people get a local reaction to bee stings, during which the area around the sting will swell and turn red. Those with allergies will get hives, facial swelling, and will have difficulty breathing.

If your child does get stung, you can run cold water on the skin and try to remove the stinger, if visible, with tweezers or by brushing it away with something stiff but pliable, like a credit card (to prevent more of the irritant in the stinger from being squeezed into the wound with tweezers). If you are at home or at a friend's house when the sting occurs, you can make a simple and soothing salve to apply to the site of the sting by mixing one teaspoon of baking soda with about one-half teaspoon of water.

Spider, Flea, and Mosquito Bites

Spiders tend to bite at night, so you'll generally notice a spider bite (a small red bump on the skin) when you're dressing your child in the morning. You might want to take his sheets and pillowcases off to wash them and look around for webs or spiders. Most spider bites aren't dangerous, but they can itch. If your child is scratching, try putting calamine lotion or a mixture of baking soda and water (mixed into a paste) on his skin. This will soothe it.

 Essential

The most effective insect repellents have a small amount of the chemical DEET in them. If you are worried about DEET on children, put a sunscreen or cream on first to decrease the risk of DEET absorption (it will still deter the bugs) or use an all-natural insect repellant.

If your animal has fleas or your child visits a house with fleas, you will need to disinfect your house and animals. Flea bites aren't dangerous, but they are annoying and itchy. There are a variety of ways to soothe itchy bites or rashes. Try applying one of the following to irritated skin:

- Calamine lotion
- Antihistamine cream
- Baking soda mixed with water
- Refrigerated rubbing alcohol or hydrogen peroxide

You can also use the above methods to soothe mosquito bites and poison ivy.

Tick Bites

If your one-year-old has been outside, you should carefully check his body, especially his scalp, for ticks, which will feel like a hard bump under your fingertips. To remove a tick, you'll need tweezers and a firm grip, so that you get the whole thing out of the skin, not just the body. (If the tick has bitten, you run the risk of removing the tick's body with tweezers, leaving the head of the tick in the skin.) If you notice a red bump and circle with a white inner circle at the site of the bite anywhere from a few days to several weeks after finding a tick, bring your child to the doctor to check for Lyme disease, which is carried by the small ticks called deer ticks. Always check your child's scalp and hairline, too, while you're washing his hair.

Poisons

A poison is anything that a child ingests that can harm or shut down his system, such as household cleaners with ammonia or bleach, liquids that go into cars (such as antifreeze and windshield washer fluid), as well as some plants and medicines. Poisons hurt the body very quickly and must be handled fast. The poison control number (1-800-222-1222) should be posted on your refrigerator and by the phone, as well as programmed into your cell phone.

If your child swallows a poison, call the poison control center or 911 and tell them exactly what your child ate or drank. If you can, read the information on the bottle to find out what you should do, but never try to bring the poison up by inducing vomiting unless you are specifically instructed to do so. Some poisons can do further damage to the child's throat when regurgitated. Instead, give your child milk (which can neutralize the poison) or water, both of which will help to "flush" the body of the poison.

If your child is unconscious, follow the resuscitation instructions on pages 177–178 while someone calls for help.

Medicine

If your child swallows or chews medicine, whether it's meant for adults or children, you'll need to call the poison control center or 911 right away. Although medicine isn't a poison, a one-year-old's body cannot tolerate medicines that aren't meant for his body or too much of any medicine.

You should know your child's height and weight (this can affect how much the medicine will affect them) so that you can quickly relay this information to the poison control representative or police dispatcher. Keep the bottle with information about the medicine near you and read what it says to the expert, who can then look up the safest and most effective remedy.

 Alert!

Aspirin is never safe for a young child. It is especially dangerous when the child has the flu or chicken pox because it is associated with a severe neurological disorder. Even the product once marketed as baby aspirin is simply a low dose of aspirin. It is no longer marketed to children but is packaged instead as an adult heart medicine.

Vitamin supplements, and especially iron pills, can be dangerous to children. Keep all medicines and supplements in a cabinet that is locked and out of reach of your child (remember that they will try to climb and reach higher shelves and medicine cabinets).

Cleaning Products

Most people keep cleaning supplies at floor level, such as under the kitchen sink or in a bucket or basket on a closet floor. With their bright colors and shiny surfaces, children love to touch the boxes, bottles, and jars that hold cleaning products. Also, because they know they aren't supposed to touch these things (and even at the age of one, they've already been told to stay away from them), they are even more intrigued by these things.

It is safer for your child—and much less stressful for you—if you simply make sure cleaning products are kept out of your one-year-old's reach. In fact, when it comes to anything that can hurt your child, out of sight, out of mind—if she can't see it, she won't want to touch or drink it.

Chapter 10

Medical Issues

Fortunately, most children these days are pictures of robust health—energetic, engaged, and well cared for. They have received their immunizations, are eating good food, and getting plenty of rest, love, and support. These are all things that help to create a strong, healthy person. Understanding how to keep your child healthy means knowing how to give him medicine, how to prevent accidents and help him recover from them, and how to deal with health issues, whether minor or serious.

Immunizations

An immunization or vaccination is a pill, drink, or shot (inoculation) that provides immunity against a disease or illness by introducing a very low dose of the virus into the individual's system. Because of the small amount of the virus, the body can successfully fight it off, creating antibodies in the process that enable the body to develop an immunity to the virus. Some immunizations are needed once, while others are "boosters," which need to be given every few years or so at intervals.

 Alert!

In addition to state-regulated required vaccinations, some pediatricians will suggest your child get a flu shot each year. Influenza is very dangerous in children, so talk to your physician about the shot and what it can do to keep your child healthy. New immunizations are coming out every year and so the schedule of shots changes, too.

While there is some controversy about immunizations (because some parents attribute inoculations to the rise in autism and other developmental delays), every parent should remember that just a few generations ago, millions of children became ill as a result of diseases such as pertussis (whooping cough) and measles which are still around today.

Before the age of five, most children will receive the following immunizations.

- Five DPT shots that protect against diphtheria, tetanus, and pertussis (also called whooping cough)
- Four polio immunizations
- Two MMR injections which protect against measles, mumps, and rubella

Your child will also likely receive three or four Hib vaccinations, which can protect a child from the bacteria that causes bacterial meningitis, epiglottitis, and blood infections, as well as other infections. Pneumococcal vaccines protect kids from ear infections, pneumonia, and meningitis. New vaccines are being developed all the time. So parents should expect changes in the vaccination schedule as new vaccines come into use.

State Regulations

Every state has its own laws about when and how often children need to be immunized against each disease. Your baby was probably first vaccinated at the hospital, just a few days after she was born. At that time, the nurse gave you a booklet or piece of paper with a list and the dates of the inoculations your baby received. This paperwork is important and you should bring it with you each time you visit the pediatrician. This is how you and the doctor (as well as any other doctors) can be sure she has been properly vaccinated.

If you move, especially to another state, your child's immunization schedule will begin to follow that state's regulation and schedule, but having the proper paperwork will ensure that she isn't over- or undervaccinated throughout her life.

Vaccination Concerns

Over the last decade or so, some parents have begun to believe there is a connection between immunizations and autism, allergies, attention deficit disorder, and some of the other issues currently affecting children. Multiple studies done in numerous countries have concluded there is no definitive link between immunizations and these health issues.

 Fact

> Autism is a word that is generally used to describe a number of disorders, including Asperger's syndrome, attachment disorder, and other problems that relate to a child's ability to connect with family and create friendships. Each of these illnesses has its own set of symptoms and treatments.

Nevertheless, if this a concern of yours, you should ask your pediatrician any questions and contact organizations (general ones are listed in Appendix A) that specialize in supporting parents whose children struggle with autism and related illnesses.

Well-Child Checkups

Young children should visit a doctor at least nine times during their first three years and at least once from twelve to twenty-four months. (Most of the visits take place soon after birth and during the first year.) While many of these visits will include immunizations, the pediatrician will also do a "well-baby check," which means he will look for signs that your baby is healthy and growing at an appropriate rate.

The doctor and his staff will weigh and measure your one-year-old to make sure she's growing at a healthy, steady rate; check her hearing and eyesight; and ask you questions about what your baby is doing, such as whether she is standing up, walking, and talking. You should also feel free to tell your doctor about your baby. The more he knows, the more he'll be able to get a realistic idea of how your baby is growing and feeling. Since a baby can't communicate with descriptive words how she is feeling, you'll want to consider and discuss certain issues with your doctor, such as these:

- How well your child sleeps
- Whether your child is eating and feeding herself (or at least trying to)
- Whether your child is drinking from a cup

If your child seems heavy or underweight, your doctor will discuss ways to fix this. The doctor will also check your child's teeth (to make sure they're coming in), and he'll try to interact with your child to see if she's engaged, curious, and happy. The doctor may ask your child a question or see if she'll point to something when asked. The doctor will see if your one-year-old's eyes follow an object (like his finger), and he'll see if she responds to voices.

Most children are healthy and developing well. Your pediatrician will be able to tell where your child is on the developmental curve. If he's concerned about something or wants you to keep an eye on a specific behavior or physical issue, he'll tell you and ask you to come back so that he can follow-up on what he's noticed. One-year-olds are often scared, over-whelmed, or preoccupied at a doctor's visit, and they don't respond exactly the way a doctor wants them to. The doctor will usually follow up with any issues at later visits to make sure your child is developing normally.

Common Problems

Few people are perfectly healthy—most people have allergies, need glasses, have eczema, or experience other minor health problems. Just as you're getting to know your child's personality, you'll also be getting to know more about her body and what she needs to be the healthiest person she can be.

Vision Issues

If your child stands very close to people or objects and puts his eyes close to them, or if he blinks, rubs his eyes, or seems surprised when you come over to him, it's possible that he has a vision problem. If he seems to notice everything, from an airplane in the sky to an ant crawling on the ground, then his vision is probably fine.

A lazy or crossed eye occurs when one eye muscle is weak or unable to focus in conjunction with the other eye. Both of these problems are usually correctable with exercises, and a doctor will notice them during a well-baby visit. Most lazy eyes are easily noticeable in the first year. Make sure your doctor checks your child's eyes during the visit.

It's difficult for a one-year-old to wear glasses, and many doctors won't prescribe them at this age because very young children might still be crawling and aren't able to keep the glasses on their heads. It's therefore very common for young children to not have the vision they will end up with—it takes a while for eye muscles to become strong.

If you notice vision problems in your baby, talk to your doctor. She will be able to test your baby with easy exercises, such as holding fingers up or moving pictures around her, and then suggest ways to help build the muscles and improve vision skills.

Ear Infections

Ear infections are one of the most common reasons parents bring their children to the doctor. This happens because the eustachian tube, which connects the middle ear to the throat, is not fully developed in one-year-olds. The eustachian tube is normally filled with air, but if a child experiences nasal congestion as a result of allergies or a cold, the underdeveloped tube can easily become blocked and filled with fluid. Germs multiply in the fluid and cause a middle-ear infection. If your child cries, pulls on her ear, or has a fever, call your doctor. Your child may be trying to communicate to you that there is pain in her ear.

If wax is a problem—if your child's hearing is affected or if his ear just looks dirty—bring him to the doctor rather than trying to go into the ear canal or doing any rinsing or deep cleaning yourself. If you clean inside the ear (with a cotton swab, for example), there is a good chance you will cause more of a problem by pushing the wax and any germs further into the ear canal. The doctor will be able to help clean it safely if necessary.

Febrile Convulsions

If your one-year-old has a viral infection with a fever, you need not fear the fever even if your family has a history of febrile convulsions, which is a shaking or stiffening of the body. Febrile (fever) convulsions (shaking) seem to be caused by a lower seizure threshold, which runs in families and which children outgrow by five years of age. These types of seizures scare people and need to be evaluated by a physician but do not cause any permanent damage. The first time your child has a febrile seizure you should take him to the emergency room so that a doctor can confirm that that is all it is and that it is not a symptom of epilepsy or a serious neurological disorder. The doctor will evaluate the symptoms and order tests to confirm that the seizure was only caused by the fever. If your child gets febrile seizures you can prevent them by careful management of the fever.

If your child has febrile convulsions, sponge her with warm to lukewarm—but never cold—water. Anything too cold will shock her body. Also, don't leave her alone or try to restrain her to stop the convulsions. Give her plenty of space and, if you can, place her on her side so that she won't choke if she vomits. Call 911 if the convulsions last more than a few minutes. These can be very scary, but be assured that most children grow out of their febrile convulsions by the time they turn five.

Colds

When they are young, children are constantly exposed to germs and viruses that their immune systems haven't yet learned how to fight off. Vomiting or a low-grade fever is not necessarily a sign of illness. Your child's ability to fight off germs with low fevers means his healthy immune system will be stronger as he gets older. Your child is truly sick when the way he feels changes the way he acts or behaves.

A cold is a virus transmitted from person to person, and there are hundreds of viruses going around at any given time. Your child's immunity to certain bugs hasn't yet been built up, so he's susceptible to a variety of colds. It's not a bad thing for a child to get a cold because over time it builds immunity to other viruses. The problem is dealing with the symptoms of a cold.

A one-year-old with a cold can be very uncomfortable and unhappy. In fact, some of his symptoms will be more behavioral than physical, such as irritability and lethargy. At the same time, with a cold, your child may still be running around and not letting himself rest.

 Essential

Call the doctor or bring your child to see him in the following cases: Your child is having trouble breathing; your child can't move a limb, or you suspect a break or fracture; your child is burned anywhere; your child has a problem with her eyes or ears; your child isn't responsive; or you are concerned with dehydration due to fluid loss.

Cold remedies are often not only unnecessary, they also don't work as they are supposed to. In fact, most cold medicines hardly do anything at all. Pseudoephedrine, for example, a common ingredient in cold medicines, can make some children hyperactive rather than relaxing them. Because a cold is a virus and is not caused by bacteria, it cannot be fought with antibiotics. You can comfort your child, but medicine will not reduce the problem. You are better off soothing the symptoms rather than trying to eliminate them.

If your baby is having trouble breathing because her nose is stuffed up, try using a nasal saline spray. You could also try bringing your child into a moist room, such as a bathroom with a hot shower running, so that she can breathe the steamy air, or into a room with a humidifier running. If she's feverish, you can give her a child's dose of acetaminophen or ibuprofen. Some doctors recommend giving one dose of acetaminophen, then alternating with ibuprofen over the course of a day to best reduce a fever, but be sure to consult your doctor before administering any medicine to your child.

Don't force your child to eat if she's not feeling well, but try to encourage her to drink water and rest. A rested body is a body that can best heal itself. Drinking enough fluids is also important because a feverish body can become dehydrated.

If you can, sit with your child while she is sick and play quietly. Read books and listen to music. But don't be afraid to take her outside and let the sun warm her. Fresh air and sunshine can only help the body repair itself and fight off a virus.

Fevers

A fever is a sign that the body is fighting an infection, so it's not unusual for children to get fevers often as their immune systems build up strength. Although low-grade fevers are common and not dangerous, you should call a pediatrician or nurse immediately if your child has a fever higher than 102°F or if it lasts more than one day. If he has other symptoms along with the fever, such as coughing, vomiting, or diarrhea, call the pediatrician's office and give a complete description of your child's behavior so the pediatrician can determine whether your child should be seen.

Don't try to reduce low-grade fevers, as fevers are a sign that the white blood cells are at work to produce antibodies that fight germs and bugs. Instead, help your baby feel more comfortable by helping her to rest. Keep her very comfortably dressed and covered while she's sleeping. If she is irritable, or the fever is making her unable to sleep, consider a fever reducer, but only enough so that she rests comfortably. Consult your doctor before using anything to reduce fever.

Medical Problems

While there is rarely a reason to panic if your child is sneezing, coughing, or has a slight fever, it does take a while to get to know how he will typically respond when he is sick. Like some adults, some children tend to get stomach bugs, while others spend all winter with runny noses, for example.

You should always bring your child to the doctor's if you're not sure what's wrong or if you're concerned about his fever or symptoms. Over time, you'll learn to recognize symptoms you can handle on your own. Often, if you simply tell the symptoms to the nurse who answers the phone, she'll be able to advise you if an office visit is necessary.

Bring your child to the doctor when she exhibits symptoms that you think might have a serious cause, such as diarrhea, coughing, vomiting, or a fever that you think may be signs of ear infection, pneumonia, or dehydration. Since you aren't a doctor, you don't want to try to diagnose these illnesses yourself. You need your doctor to explain how to treat them.

The number-one way to tell if you should see a doctor is if your child is acting differently than usual. Lethargy, intense unhappiness and crying, or other behaviors that you can't soothe or figure out means a professional might need to diagnose the problem. Specific symptoms, such as ear pulling or a severe cough, are signs that you need a doctor's diagnosis.

Fevers, cough, runny nose, and an upset stomach are all symptoms that will make some sense to you. While you may choose to bring your child to the doctor when these things occur, you don't necessarily need to do that. You need to have the right medicines and know how to treat common illnesses.

Medicine Cabinet

Your medicine cabinet should include first-aid treatments; cold, flu, and cough soothers (remember, you can't cure them); and other items that keep a body healthy. You should have the following on hand:

- Adhesive bandages of all shapes and sizes
- Antibiotic cream and antiseptic wipes
- Antifungal cream and anti-itch cream
- Diaper rash ointment
- A thermometer (digital thermometer as well as mercury/rectal one)
- Saline spray
- Syrup of ipecac
- Pepto-Bismol and gas reliever

- Pedialyte
- Sunscreen with an SPF of 15 or higher

Be sure to tell your pediatrician about any medicines you give your baby. If she gives you a prescription, be sure you follow the instructions. Once you have administered the medicine according to the instructions, throw any that is left over away.

Fever Reducers

As you've read, low-grade fevers are not necessarily dangerous and don't need to be treated if your child isn't uncomfortable. However, you should always have fever reducers on hand just in case. They should include ibuprofen and acetaminophen as opposed to aspirin or aspirin derivatives, which can make children very sick. Always check the expiration dates on medications. Beyond those dates, they won't help your child.

Painkillers

Most fever reducers, including ibuprofen and acetaminophen, are also painkillers. You should use these if your child has growing pains and is very uncomfortable, or if she has hurt herself and can't ignore the pain.

 Fact

Growing pains are real and usually occur at night. A child may wake up with pains in his legs or hips. If your child has pains that make him limp or otherwise curtail his daily activity, take him to the doctor for an evaluation.

One-year-olds don't yet know how to cope with pain and illness, so you are doing your child a favor if you talk her through the experience, explaining that relaxing, doing something to keep her mind occupied, and taking long deep breaths can do a lot to alleviate any feelings of discomfort. You don't want to give your child medicine too easily or for every small thing. For one thing, overmedication is dangerous and can cause other complications.

Decongestants and Cough Remedies

Medicines that reduce cold and flu symptoms by drying up the nasal passages have many side effects and should only be used as a last resort. They don't cure the underlying problem, which is a virus, and they often don't have a clear and effective way to help the body to do what it needs to in order to heal.

Very few cough "remedies" actually work, and many have ingredients that have unpleasant side effects, such as edginess and irritability. Look for cough remedies that do not contain pseudoephedrine. Often, the most soothing remedies for a cough are frequent sips of warm water with honey and lemon, sitting upright, and plenty of rest.

Administering Medicine

If you do need to give medicine to your child, you'll most likely find it in flavored liquid form, such as grape or cherry. This makes the medicine appealing to your child, and he won't put up a fight to avoid taking it.

New forms of medication include strips that melt on a child's tongue, which are fine for most one-year-olds, but others may have an allergy to leuketrines, which is one of the ingredients that make the strips melt. Check to be sure, too, that the over-the-counter remedy you give your child doesn't contain alcohol. Always check the package directions and follow the dosage recommendations based on your child's weight, a more exact method than following age recommendations. And if you are giving your child more than one type of medicine, speak to your doctor about whether there is a danger of complications resulting from the mixed medicines.

Avoiding Infections

The best thing you can do for your baby is to help him not get sick in the first place. This isn't always easy, as children very easily catch germs and don't have strong immune systems to fight them off. However, you can do a number of things to help your child stay clean, which is the best way to fight infections.

The Basics of Infection

Infections are virus germs that make their way into the body through the nose, eyes, and mouth. People usually come into contact with viruses by touching something contaminated with their hands, and they become infected by putting their hands into their nose, eyes, or mouth. This is why it's so important to wash your hands—and your baby's hands—often. Antibacterial wipes are great for this, because you don't have to use a public restroom or get your child into the bathroom of your house to clean her up.

If someone physically close to your one-year-old is sick, whether it's an adult or a child, be sure that person doesn't breathe, cough, or sneeze near your child. Unfortunately, you have to rely on other parents to keep their sick children home from day care and to cancel play dates when necessary. This is sometimes awkward, as not all parents are equally responsible about protecting the health of other children. If you suspect a child is sick and you want to keep your child away from her, you'll need to tell the other parent that you don't want to expose your child to a virus.

It is up to you to stay on top of the situation. If you need to, ask the other parent why the child is coughing or sneezing and if they are using medicine. If you feel that your child is being exposed to a virus or germs, you'll need to wipe off her hands and mouth, and any toys the children have shared.

Disinfecting

While cleaning is helpful, overcleaning, especially with antibiotic cleansers, is actually too much of a good thing. There are such things as healthy germs, and those germs fight infections and viruses. If you overclean your baby and your house, you will also get rid of the infection-fighting elements. Cleanliness is important because it does reduce the risk of infection and illness, but recent research has shown that overcleaning can actually lead to other, more serious illnesses, such as asthma. This is because a healthy body develops a healthy immune system when it encounters and fights off common germs.

In fact, the best things you can clean in order to keep your child healthy are toys she shares with other children. Simply wipe them down with a damp washcloth (using just a little bit of soap) and let them dry. You do not need to boil toys or use an antiseptic or antibacterial cleanser on them.

Chapter 11

Common Concerns

How is a one-year-old supposed to act? You may worry when your child can't sit still in a restaurant, but that is perfectly normal for a one-year-old. You may worry when he lies in his crib for an entire hour babbling to himself and playing with his feet. But that, too, is entirely normal. Rest assured, from quiet to loud, from brave to frightened, from calm to moody, most of the behavior you'll see this year will fall into the "entirely normal" range.

Overcoming Shyness

Even the most naturally outgoing child will have moments of self-consciousness and shyness. It's important for parents to realize that children are negotiating their interaction with the outside world and new people all the time. It is natural for them to sometimes feel shades of self-consciousness and shyness.

Shyness is a genetic trait, so if you do have a shy child, there is a good chance that you or your partner is also shy. If you feel your shyness has been detrimental in your life, you may want to discourage your child from being shy, but you need to be aware of how your reaction to her personality will feel to her. If she's shy, don't tease, pressure, or admonish her about her feelings. Instead, guide her through her first interactions with strangers. Empathy rather than discipline will help her most. Expressing confidence in her and her abilities will work better then verbal pressure.

Personality

Although there is plenty of reason (and research) to believe that the way your child is raised will affect his developing personality, there is just as much research to support the idea that much of his personality is genetic. Therefore, you'll need to watch your child as you help him navigate each new situation. What makes him worried? Where does he feel confident? Is he someone who tries something then finds himself in the midst of a situation and looks around for you? Or is he cautious and hesitant at first, slowly gaining an understanding of the experience and then relaxing enough to take part and interact with others?

Effective parents release their expectations (which all parents have) and get to know their child as an individual. Then, they support their child as they develop and grow, using the child as a guide. The child doesn't have control, of course, but the parent attempts to understand and always respects their child as his or her own separate person.

 Fact

> There is no one right personality, and every child has his own level of energy, empathy, attachment, and communicativeness. He may be pretty much the same from day to day, or he may go up and down, with fluctuating moods and energy levels.

Confidence

Recognizing that all situations are new to a one-year-old, parents can do a lot to help their children develop confidence and good behavior skills. First, you can describe to your child the event you're going to or the experience he's about to have. "We're going to visit Mommy's office. When we get there, we'll go in the elevator, and then we'll say hi to Mommy's friend, Debbie. Then we're going out to lunch at a restaurant with Debbie."

Respecting a child's need to know is a new concept. For many years, parents, teachers, and other experts assumed that children were blank slates and that they could simply be trained to behave well by a system of reward and punishment as well as repeated instruction. But now we know that the most confident and happy children have secure boundaries—they know their parents have ultimate control and are the bosses—but they also feel respected and valued for who they are at every given age.

Your child may not understand or remember all the information you give, but it will give him a sense of security as he encounters what you had previously explained to him. He won't know how to behave just because you told him what he was going to encounter; however, as he gets older, he will come to rely on such information to better prepare himself for daily schedules and events.

Avoiding Shame

While many parents would never dream of hitting their children, they don't realize just how much the wrong words can hurt a child. One-year-olds do not know right from wrong, and almost all of them want nothing more than to please their moms and dads. When you tell your baby that she is wrong or bad, she doesn't realize you are talking about her behavior and not her, the person. Telling a baby she is bad makes her think there is something inherently wrong with her and that she is an unlovable person.

Do your best to offer your child explanations and instructions without commenting negatively on her. For example, imagine your one-year-old spills her milk. Rather than saying, "You are so clumsy! I can't even trust you to keep the table clean," you can say, "Oh, it's hard to learn how to hold a cup. Next time, we'll put less milk in so that it's not so heavy and you can try to drink it more slowly." After you offer her instruction, let her know how happy and proud you are of the way she is growing up. This will allow her to accept herself as she is and not feel insecure as she grows up.

Aggression

What adults label aggression is really unintentional behavior in a small child. In other words, a one-year-old will not hit or bite in a premeditated way; she will only do so because she hasn't yet learned to use words to communicate. You'll need to remember that aggressive behavior in a one-year-old—hitting, biting, kicking, or yelling—is not necessarily a sign that a child has an aggressive personality. It is simply an early behavior form that all children try to see if it works.

 Essential

One good way to look at phases is to consider all negative behavior as a phase (or a chance for instruction) and all positive behavior as a reality, that is, the person your child really is. Then, react expressively (with emotion) to positive behavior, but react with detachment, without emotion, to phase behavior.

One of the most interesting developmental occurrences you'll notice is "the phase." A phase is a period during which your child will repeat a certain behavior or behavioral style. For example, she may yell more than usual for a few weeks or may be extra sweet and calm. It's amazing how suddenly a phase will come along and then how suddenly it will leave.

When your child begins to behave in a way that is surprising to you, and if she continues the behavior, it's best to relax your expectations for a short time in order to determine if the behavior is just a phase.

You should always, of course, react to your child and take an interest, but don't judge what she's doing as if her future depends on her behavior today. Chances are she's trying on a new behavior to determine what your reaction will be. If you overreact, she might find the behavior more intriguing. If you react with instruction, but little emotion, she'll see that it's not worth her time.

Childhood Obesity

In one of the most dangerous developments over the last few years, an extraordinary number of children now struggle with their weight, and that problem can begin as early as infancy. Lifestyle changes are almost entirely to blame for this problem. Watching too much television, eating processed foods, and not having active time are some of the behaviors at fault for the childhood obesity epidemic.

Diet

There is no reason for a young child (or an adult for that matter) to eat or drink sodas, processed snack foods, and candy. Fruit and calcium-rich foods make the best snacks. Unlike older children, one-year-olds rely on you completely for the food choices. If they are eating poorly or are not active enough, you need to make their lifestyle changes for them.

Childhood obesity is dangerous for a number of reasons. First, it sets a baby up for a lifetime of health problems and weight struggle. An overweight child is more likely to be overweight as an adult and to struggle with weight-related illnesses such as diabetes and cardiovascular problems. Second, overweight children develop habits that will make it more difficult for them to eat well and exercise more as they get older. Third, their childhood will be more difficult, including potential illness, as well as school problems due to poor nutrition and a lack of healthy physical development.

Genetics

Some children are genetically predisposed to weight problems. If the adults in your family were heavy as children, then your child may struggle with this, too. If obesity runs in your family, tell your pediatrician. She should be able to help you find ways to feed your child well. When an entire family is overweight, it is even more important to emphasize a healthy diet.

 Alert!

The more the television is on, the more likely it is that your child will be overweight. Whether your child watches television is completely within your control. Though most children under the age of two watch more than two hours of television a day, they are perfectly happy without the television at all.

Even if exercise and an active lifestyle do not come naturally to you or your family, you will do your child a great favor in life if you get outside to play with him, and do things like go to the pool and run around playgrounds. Activity is a significant contributor to good health, and all parents should encourage their children to engage in it.

Early Potty Training

While some parents swear that they have their children potty trained at six months or a year, this is very rare and, experts would say, not true potty training. In other words, it is rare that a one-year-old can identify when she needs to use the bathroom, can get herself to the bathroom in time and handle her clothes, and then do what she needs to. For one thing, most one-year-olds can't readily manipulate their clothes. For another, they rarely have the bodily control to "hold it" when necessary.

If early toilet training is important to you, it is possible to control how and when your children go to the bathroom—even though there is no reason to do this. For example, you can sit them on the potty at specific times of the day, let's say, twenty minutes after they've eaten, and stay with them until they've done something. Or, you could bring them to the potty every half hour or so and see if something happens.

But, once again, if you're doing most of the work—determining when they're going—then they really aren't toilet-trained. In fact, you may be setting up a battle in an area where the child has ultimate control. It's her body. She's going to figure that out sooner, not later.

There is no intellectual, emotional, or psychological benefit to early toilet training. No evidence has shown that children who are toilet trained early are smarter or more well-adjusted than other children.

Potty-Training Readiness

Despite there being no reason to potty train your child this year, you may see signs that he is interested in trying to sit on the toilet or a potty seat. You should feel free to get a potty seat for him to sit on. In fact, your best bet is a potty seat that goes on the floor, so that your one-year-old can get on and off of it himself.

If your child shows an interest in taking off his diaper or watching you use the bathroom, then you should encourage him, as these are signs that he might be ready to use a toilet. Also, if he's happy to sit on the potty, then that's a sign of potty-training readiness.

Potty-Training Methods

At twelve to twenty-four months, you can use support and time to help potty train your baby, but it is not the time to offer rewards for potty training. Your child may regress back to diapers, and you don't want her to feel that she has begun to do something wrong if that happens. If it does happen, you should remain completely calm about it, as the less pressure you put on your child, the more likely it is that she'll return to her good habits.

The best thing to do for a child this age is to encourage, not pressure, her to experiment with the potty. You can put the potty on the floor and let her copy you when you use the bathroom without bringing her over to it. Make the experience lighthearted, with no pressure. If she gets up without doing anything, tell her she did a good job for trying.

Developmental Delays

Every child has his own way of growing, learning, and expressing himself, which is why doctors look at a range of behaviors and growth patterns when determining how well a child is developing. A symptom, such as not having made any type of speech sound by the time a child is eighteen months old, might signify any of a variety of problems, but this may also be a case of a quiet child who is waiting to speak until he has something to say.

If you wonder if your baby is having trouble reaching a milestone or taking a step in his development, take him to the doctor and explain your concern. The most likely result of your conversation will be that you feel reassured about your concern. If otherwise, your pediatrician should be able to guide you to getting a full developmental assessment.

Signs of Developmental Delays

Sometimes parents notice behavior that makes them worry. Maybe their baby doesn't respond or smile, does the same thing over and over again for hours, doesn't seem as happy or engaged as other babies, or seems clumsier or more awkward than other babies. They wonder what this behavior means.

All of these are valid concerns and represent the types of behavioral signs parents should take seriously. Developmental delays can be helped with early intervention. Don't let fear of what you will find out stop you from asking questions and seeing specialists; their help can make a difference in how your child learns and grows.

Developmental delays can affect children in a variety of areas, such as physical, emotional, or intellectual. Some delays can be worked on and then evened out, while others will be a lifetime issue. Discovering a problem early makes addressing and adapting to it that much easier.

Seven Types of Intelligence

Sometimes, a delay in learning some skills, such as speaking or walking, can overshadow an early development of other abilities. Even a one-year-old child can demonstrate an interest and preference for some activities over others, which can be a signal that she has an aptitude for a certain style of learning or a specific skill. Your one-year-old may love shaking maracas or banging a pot on the floor, or perhaps she'll take apart all the toys you give her but never seem interested in crayons. Whatever her interests, she is likely showing a form of development that is characteristic of one of the many types of intelligence.

Parents tend to focus on certain ages and milestones (such as first words and first steps) as signs that their child is smart and will grow up to be normal. But experts no longer believe intelligence is a stand-alone quality. For this reason, many experts believe that there is no one right way for children to develop and learn. For example, while one child may walk for a few months before he says his first word, another child may speak fairly intelligibly but still cling to the furniture in order to make his way around the room.

To explain these types of development more specifically, Howard Gardner of the Massachusetts Institute of Technology developed a theory that there are seven types of intelligence:

- **Spatial:** Block building, stacking cups, and even knocking down blocks and toys are signs of spatial development.
- **Musical:** If your child immediately starts moving to music or likes to bang on the furniture or pots and pans, she is developing her musical intelligence.
- **Kinetic:** Dancing, walking, and playing with toys are all signs of kinetic intelligence, something that athletes and dancers must have.
- **Interpersonal:** Is your child laughing and smiling at you? When you play peek-a-boo, does she respond? This is interpersonal intelligence—she's bonding and interacting.
- **Linguistic:** Early talkers and children who understand big words and concepts are gifted linguistically. These children may grow up to enjoy writing, and they also love to be read to.
- **Logical-mathematic:** This may be hard to recognize at a very young age, but children who enjoy sorting (dividing blocks by colors or size) are often showing an early mathematical gift. Logical thinking may show itself by understanding that a ball is under a pillow or knowing where to look for lost toys.
- **Intrapersonal:** This type of intelligence relates to self-awareness and self-wisdom. It may seem that a young child has little self-awareness, but if your child can point to what hurts or even attempts to tell you he doesn't like the dinner you made him, he is expressing self-awareness.

This theory has been widely accepted by the psychological and educational communities so that teaching and learning styles can be adapted to children with all types of gifts. No one type of intelligence is more important or more valuable than another, and all of them should be valued and encouraged. You'll notice, though, that your child's natural interests and gifts fall in some categories more than others. That doesn't mean she won't have some skills in every category—we all do. It simply means that you'll notice she, like all of us, enjoys and develops some skills more readily than others.

Of course, no matter what their level of intelligence in any area, children need to be taught and coached in order to grow and learn more. Appreciating your child's abilities and interests will not only allow her to develop those gifts, but to feel confident.

 Fact

Gifted children, who make up about 2 percent of the population, also need special attention; if they aren't stimulated, their boredom can manifest itself as behavior problems. Gifted children tend to like older children and adults, and they often have early language skills. They are often bored by repetition and have long attention spans for their age.

All children need their parents and educators to teach them in ways that work for their individual skills and talents, no matter where they fall on the developmental continuum. In fact, even children who were once previously thought of as physically or mentally challenged are now rewarded and appreciated for their gifts through programs such as Special Olympics. Therefore, if you are told your child has a developmental delay at this early age, you might try to look for specialists and support groups that aim to encourage young children to develop any gifts they might have.

Autism

Most children respond early in life to their parent's voices and then begin to smile and react to other people and sounds, as well as images and sights. A very small percentage of children, however, don't respond and seem not to bond with their parents. They remain isolated and often practice a lot of repetitive behavior, such as tapping or banging. When they learn to speak, children with autism may simply repeat a word over and over without seeming to communicate.

 Essential

Autism is in no way a reflection on a parent's ability to love and nurture her child, as it was once believed to be. If your child is diagnosed with a developmental delay such as autism, you might consider joining a support group or talking to a therapist to gain support and clarity on how you can handle this situation.

Autism is actually a spectrum of disorders (which includes Asperger's syndrome) involving language and social development. It does not have to isolate a child and can be handled with clear thinking and rational help. It has been about twenty-five years since children began to be more commonly diagnosed with autism and Asperger's, and many of the young adults who lived with these conditions have become fully functional, capable grownups.

Signs and Symptoms

Aside from rocking and seeming disconnected, your child may seem overly focused on one detail of a toy or not be able to play with a toy in new ways, such as using a spoon to bang and then stir and then build with. No exact cause for autism is known, but research is pointing toward a genetic predisposition to certain behaviors and thinking patterns. In fact, some families have other children with developmental delays and other disorders along the autism spectrum.

Getting a Diagnosis

If you are worried that your twelve- to twenty-four-month-old child is showing signs of autism or any of the autism spectrum disorders, the first person to talk to is your child's primary pediatrician. If this doctor has known your baby since birth, she will easily detect developmental delays and be able to respond to your concerns if you feel your child isn't thriving emotionally or intellectually.

You might want to write down what you notice about your child's behavior so that you are well prepared to answer any questions the doctor may have for you while determining a diagnosis. For example, if you notice your son recoils from your touch or seems to be lost in his own world, or if your daughter can't adjust to new surroundings or change, then that is something to tell your doctor.

Your pediatrician will compare your child's behavior to diagnostics guidelines established by the American Academy of Child and Adolescent Psychiatry (AACAP). She may also schedule your child for hearing, vision, and other tests to rule out other health concerns.

Keeping your pediatrician informed about your concerns, and making sure she is also looking out for signs and symptoms of delays, will help your child in the future, too. If your child is two or slightly older and still lagging behind, you can offer this information to a specialist who can make an accurate diagnosis based on your child's current and past behaviors. Doctors and specialists can offer parents ideas on communication, behavioral training, and other therapeutic skills that can improve a child's health outlook.

Although no parent causes or is responsible for any of the autism spectrum disorders, it is true that early intervention can help. Working with a team, whether it's only your primary care physician or a primary care physician along with a specialist, will help you and your child pursue a healthy future.

Chapter 12

Fun and Games

This year of your child's life will likely be one full of fun, as one-year-olds are curious about the world around them and are always eager to try new things. They are naturally excited about learning. One of the joys of having a young child in your home is that everything is play for them. Play is a child's work in that it helps them learn. While many adults think learning is something they should do to better themselves, for a one-year-old, learning can be fun, playful, engaging, and interesting.

Pretend Play

At one, many children will do a lot of imitative play. They love to use plastic cell phones, pretend to shop, and dress up and wear costumes, all trying to act like mom and dad. They will want to use your pots and pans to pretend to cook and will serve you imaginary food on plastic plates and dishes.

 Essential

Girls and boys alike, at this age, will enjoy playing with baby dolls. They like to pretend they are moms and dads and take care of their babies—feeding them, washing them, and even reprimanding them. This is an example of the imitative play that one-year-olds love.

Pretend play is like memorization for a one-year-old. It reminds her about her world and the course of her day. By acting like her mom, dad, or teacher, she is experiencing her life from a different point of view, and this helps her mind grow.

The Beginning of Imagination

One-year-olds are only beginning to use their imagination as a tool for play. Their play won't be dramatic (as in creating story lines or with a lot of fantasy), and they won't be able to play with another child in an imaginative way quite yet. In other words, a fifteen-month-old may say to another child his own age, "You be the mommy and I'll be the daddy," but the two of them will not be able to extend that play out into developing a story line. Instead, they will simply feed the baby, wash the baby, or dress the baby. They may repeat these behaviors over and over again to make sure they get it right.

How Imagination Helps Development

Many parents think fantasy is not as important to learning because it is pretend and not real, but brain development in a young child takes place in a variety of ways. First, she learns adult behavior by taking on the role of a grownup when she cares for her dolls or stuffed animals. Second, she develops empathy and emotional intelligence by taking care of her toys. Third, her brain creates connections when it is engaged in imaginative thought. Creativity—brainstorming, thinking of solutions to problems, and imagination—is a true hallmark of intelligence, so it is important for parents to encourage this type of play. Children don't need much to be creative. Cardboard boxes, pots and pans, paper plates, a few dolls or stuffed animals, and blocks can become houses, a kitchen, a school, and a trip to the grocery store.

Play Dates

If your child isn't in day care and thus isn't playing with and in contact with children for much of the day, or if she doesn't have siblings, she may benefit from short play dates with other children. (Of course, even if she is in these situations, you can feel free to arrange play dates for her.) While children at this age mostly take part in parallel play—that is, not interacting as much as doing similar activities while next to each other—they still enjoy being near each other and watching each other.

If you can, be sure there are at least two of each toy the children will get to play with when they are together. One-year-olds cannot share. If they see another child playing with a toy, that is the one they will want. If a dispute arises over a toy, it is often easiest to distract them with another attractive item. Rather than point it out to them, simply start playing with something else. Your attention to another toy will be intriguing to them.

 Fact

The most important thing to remember about play dates for one-year-olds is that one-year-olds are easily distracted and don't have a lot of patience for extensive interaction with each other. They only need an hour or two (at the most) of time together before they begin to want attention for themselves.

Also, if possible, at this age, you are probably better off keeping both moms or dads around for the visit, unless the child knows and feels comfortable with the parent of the other child. Finally, remember that one-year-olds cannot entertain each other. They will need you to be part of their time together and will look to you for ideas and interaction.

Choosing Safe Toys

If you head to a toy store, you'll notice most children's toys are large, bright, and plastic. When your child bangs them (and he will) nothing breaks or flies off. The age-appropriateness of the toy will be indicated right on the packaging, and that is information you should take seriously. Small pieces of toys designed for older children can be dangerous to a young child.

Many parents believe they will be giving their children an intellectual head start if they buy toys that are labeled "educational," even though there is absolutely no proof or research that shows these toys are in any way effective or useful. These products are usually expensive and often electronic.

If you have toys from an older child or from your child, make sure there are no broken parts. If they are made of wood, be sure it isn't splintered and that anything that connects parts isn't loose. Beware of your older child's Legos, dolls with little shoes, and any toys that disassemble and have small parts because of the potential danger of your child choking on these small items. A good way to test whether something is a choking hazard is to slide it through a cardboard paper towel tube. If the item fits in the tube opening, it is a potential choking hazard.

The best toys for young children are often the least complicated. They can include instruments, play-dough, chalk for the sidewalk, soft balls, blocks, and dolls.

Boxes

Many parents have joked about how they will buy their child a gift only to find the child is more interested in the box than in the actual toy. Knowing that boxes are endlessly enticing to children is good because it gives you an understanding of what appeals to one-year-olds. Similar toys include small buckets (which can often be stacked if they are of different sizes), pails and shovels, and plastic containers (just make sure the containers can't fit over their heads or in their mouths.)

 Alert!

If you give your child a large box, such as the size a refrigerator comes in, make sure it can't close completely and that your child is able to get out of it. You might try cutting a hole in it, so it can be a rocket ship or house. If your child climbs into it, make sure she won't fall while she's in it.

At this age, babies like to put things in and take things out of boxes, so give her socks, balls, or spoons with a box and she'll be entertained for a while. Or, give her various boxes of different sizes, such as shoe and boot boxes. She'll make them into beds for her dolls, as well as other pretend things.

Another helpful item for children is fabric or old clothes of yours. Blankets, scarves, vests, dresses, and even just fabric scraps can become tents, pretend clothes, places to have a picnic, or the sails of boats (especially when paired with a box).

Play Phases

Use your child as a guide to what he wants to play with. If he finds your dresser drawer fascinating, give him a place in your room for clothes he can play with. If he loves the kitchen, designate a cabinet for his use in which he has pots, dishes, and utensils to use. If he always wants to splash in water, don't hesitate to let him take a bath in the middle of the day. Play phases, like food and behavior phases, have their place in a child's development. Your child will eventually grow tired of each new interest, but in the meantime these phases serve a learning purpose.

Television

In many homes, the television is on for a large portion of the day. Parents fall asleep with a television on, televisions are in every room, and there are dozens of shows, even on educational channels, that are marketed as being appropriate and educational for young babies.

The amount of television watching you and your child do is directly related to weight problems, mood disorders such as depression, and to feelings of anxiety. A recent study concluded that early television viewing is associated with attention difficulties during school years. It is important for all parents to monitor the presence of television in their lives and in the lives of their one-year-olds, because it doesn't only affect their lives now, but their health and wellness later on.

Keep in mind that television recommendations include computer, video, and DVD time, not just time spent watching television shows. The information is intended to cover all passive screen time, as there is no developmental reason for a child to sit in front of any type of machine.

Docs Say No

Officially, the American Academy of Pediatrics (AAP) does not recommend television for children aged two or younger. Your one-year-old will not want the television on for any reason of her own, although that will change if you make it appealing to her. If you can, keep it off while she's in the room. You may think that she's oblivious to its sights and sounds, but the truth is, she is aware of what's going on even though she can't process the adult information in any kind of meaningful way.

According to Nielsen Reports, children in the United States watch about four hours of television every day. They also see many commercials during children's programs for unhealthy foods, such as candy, snacks, sugary cereals, and drinks that can lead them to desire these products as they get older.

While it may seem like the television is on for just a few minutes, in reality, the effect is cumulative. The average child sees more than 20,000 commercials each year. If your child watches three to four hours of noneducational television per day, he will have seen about 8,000 TV murders by the time he finishes grade school.

Real Life Says Maybe

Of course, the reality is that you're going to turn the TV on sometimes, and you may even turn on a movie or television show designed specifically for a young child. Real life happens. If you need to take an important phone call or do something, chances are you will look for something that captures your child's attention for a few minutes. Studies have shown that high-quality, nonviolent children's shows can have a positive effect on learning.

If you're going to turn the television on, make sure it's tuned to public television or playing a DVD designed for a young baby. These often feature classical music with pictures of animals, which aren't aggressive in any way.

Physical Activity

Look up boundless bundles of energy in the dictionary, and maybe you'll see a picture of your very favorite one-year-old—shoving toys in her mouth, crawling across the floor to chase the dog, taking every item out of the bottom drawer in the bathroom, and ripping every tissue out of the box. Even if they can't walk, toddlers don't stop moving. While it may seem as though you don't need to direct your child to move, there are ways you can help him learn through active play.

The first things you need are realistic expectations about what physical skills a one-year-old has and what he doesn't. For example, one-year-olds can't do any of these things:

- Hop and skip
- Walk backward
- Throw with any aim or accuracy
- Jump
- Catch

One-year-olds can, however, *try* to do all of these things, and they will try if they see you doing them. Whatever you play with your child, treat her as an equal in terms of respect, if not skill. Accept her intellectual ability and praise her for trying and for playing. This is a good time for you to have fun because of the effort being made rather than any achievement. The point, after all, is to have fun.

In addition to spending time in active play with your one-year-old, you should also try to engage her mentally with the world around her. You can do this in any kind of everyday situation, such as when you take a walk, go to the grocery store, meet with friends, or go to the zoo. You can point out objects and note their colors or names. You could say, for example, "See the blue bird?" or "The rubber duckie is yellow!" You shouldn't expect her to know these things or to be able to communicate them to you, as much of the feedback she gives you will come not from understanding but from rote memorization. But in a year or so, she'll be able to make connections and understand what yellow or a duck really is.

Learning should be fun at this age. In fact, it shouldn't really be considered learning as much as exposure. Whether it's playing, looking at animals, reading a book, or taking a walk outside, what your child experiences at one is more significant to her development than what she communicates to you about her understanding. At this point, she is absorbing more than she is able to express.

Reading to Your One-Year-Old

Chances are there will be someone in your life who asks you why you read to your one-year-old. Many people assume that a child as young as one cannot understand what you are reading to him about or what the pictures in the storybook mean. But more and more research has shown that exposing your children to books as early as possible—just like exposing them to all types of words and experiences—will only help them love reading and books as they get older.

One of the best times to read to your child is before nap-time or bedtime. Lie down on the bed or hold him on your lap. One or two short books will be enough, and books written and designed for children this age *are* short, so this only takes about ten minutes and will be a relaxing and enjoyable part of your day and your child's day. Another way to incorporate reading into your one-year-old's life is to bring her to the library. Many bookstores also often have story hours for children.

 Fact

You can tell your baby stories instead of relying on a book as a form of entertainment. However, the act of reading—looking at and making sense of words and pictures—is a specific skill that requires practice. Going to the library and bookstores, and letting your child see you read, will encourage him to explore reading as he gets older.

Reading picture books is important at this age because your child will begin to make connections between what she's looking at and your words—and maybe even the text she sees on the page, although that probably won't happen for a few years.

While you read to your baby, point to the picture, even if it's the only thing on the page. Eventually, she'll mimic this and, over time, make the connection between your words and what she's looking at.

Some picture books designed for babies have a noun and a verb ("Worms wiggle") or noun and adjective or adverb

("Wiggly worms") with each picture. You should feel free to act out the action and respond to the text. The more animated you are as you read, the more you will entice and engage your baby.

Bring board books along in the car or diaper bag, but try to find larger size books for reading at home, as the bigger pictures are easier for a one-year-old to see.

Music

Singing and dancing are instincts. All humans—and many animals—respond to music. In fact, you probably started singing to your child soon after she was born because the sound of your voice was instantly soothing to her. You also may have noticed that your baby responds to different types of music with movement or nodding or even trying to sing.

While it's perfectly fine to play your own music for your baby, you might want to try finding music created specifically for children, as the particular sounds are often more pleasant for young ears (higher notes and less complicated tunes). Also, as they get a little older, children will become more aware of the words to the songs. Children often have trouble distinguishing the words in grown-up songs and will find the simple thoughts in kids' music more engaging.

Creating Music

Even at the age of one, your child can bang a drum, shake bells, and hit a xylophone or press buttons that make noises. You should encourage this activity with your child. It is an early way for him to experience cause and effect, as well as enjoy the process of making music. One great, inexpensive instrument for young children is the Egg, an egg-shaped toy with little beads inside that makes a rattling noise when you shake it. These cost around $1 and young children love to shake them.

If you want, you can also make your own instruments. Children can bang on pots and they can ring any type of bell. You can also put beans in a coffee can with a removable plastic lid and have your child shake it. If you have an old instrument in your house, such as a guitar or violin, that you don't mind getting slightly damaged, keep it on the floor so your child can explore it. Don't expect a one-year-old to "play" anything, though. If you can, let your one-year-old play with the instrument incorrectly, too, so that he doesn't feel intimidated or uncomfortable but rather feels confident and enjoys the experience.

Ways to Use Music

Turning on music for a baby is wonderfully stimulating—and sometimes soothing—for him. Just as you put on different music to match your moods, you should remember that loud music will keep him awake while gentle music will help him fall asleep.

Here's a great trick. When you're trying to change your wriggly baby's diaper, start to sing. Pick a new song each time or stick to an old favorite (see the list in Appendix B); chances are your baby will relax and start to sing with you. One-year-olds love to sing. Teach her the A-B-C song, "Twinkle, Twinkle, Little Star," "She'll Be Coming 'Round the Mountain," or even the chorus to your rock and roll favorites ("Yellow Submarine" is a good one). She'll get a smile on her face in no time.

Whether you choose to play games, sing songs, read together, or participate in all of these activities, spending time with your one-year-old is the most important thing you can do to ensure that you will raise a happy and healthy child. The journey from twelve to twenty-four months has its challenging moments, but for an involved and engaged parent it will be a very special time that is more about giggles and hugs, fun and play than almost anything else. There is nothing quite like having a toddler in the house. They are so excited by the smallest things in life, like bugs, a cookie, dancing, their blanket, and, most especially, you—the person who loves them and takes care of them. The gift of your time and interest will be rewarded each time they look at you with love and trust.

Appendix A

Further Resources

This section lists Web sites and books that can give you more information about one-year-old children. Understanding as much as possible about your one-year-old will help you make informed decisions abut her health and development, but it's important to remember that your confidence in your own understanding and intuition about your child's needs are just as valuable to her well-being as a doctor's advice.

Web Sites

Remember that not everything you read on the Internet has been researched, proven, or vetted by a physician or pediatrician. Also, the parents who give advice on blogs or boards are not people who know you or your child.

The following Web sites are all reputable and reliable, although the information on any of their blogs or boards is not necessarily reviewed by a physician or expert.

You can personalize a lot of these sites to the exact age of your child, so that each month you receive an e-newsletter explaining how your baby is growing and changing.

✑*www.ivillage.com*

Click on the parenting tab, then find the age of your child to read more about all sorts of issues, including reliable health information, quizzes, nutrition, and recipes, as well as shopping and crafts. Some of this information comes from magazines associated with iVillage.com, including *Good Housekeeping* and *Redbook*.

✑*www.parenting.com*

From *Parenting* magazine, the information on this Web site includes articles from the past that are age-specific, including each month between twelve and twenty-four months, which is then broken down into health, nutrition, and other categories.

✑*www.child.com*

Here you'll find short, informative articles, as well as timely stories. This site is much more like a traditional magazine than others. Includes cultural information (such as the ten best museums for kids) and a "daily laugh," as well as health, wellness, and developmental items.

✎*www.familyfun.com*

This is the Web site to go to for crafts, activities, and creative ideas, as well as timely recipes (for holidays) and birthday party ideas. It's also useful for vacation suggestions.

✎*www.aap.org*

This is the Web site of the American Academy of Pediatrics, which is designed for parents and doctors. You can search for information by age or topic, and the information is highly reliable, although it is written in a dry manner. Nevertheless, it is a great resource for health information.

✎*www.parents.com*

Articles and q-and-a's from *Parents* magazine, arranged by age as well as subject matter. This site is a little more plain—and thus easier to navigate—than the other magazine Web sites. The advice and information is reliable and given by both doctors and parents.

✎*www.childrensdefense.org*

An important advocacy group for children and those who care for them, the Children's Defense Fund Web site has information about how government programs and funding affects children and children's programs. The organization is especially helpful to families with limited incomes and resources who need to have their voices heard by the government.

✑www.webmd.com

This site is full of helpful information for people of all ages, but you can go to its "parenting and family" page for extensive facts and advice on a wide variety of childhood illnesses and behavior issues. There are physician and parent blogs, as well as q-and-a's and a "symptom checker" page.

✑www.zerotothree.org

This is the Web site for the national organization that supports the healthy development of babies and toddlers. Includes basic developmental information, as well as information on the lobbying this organization does to help fund programs for children.

Books

The following books are for parents.

First Meals: The Complete Cookbook and Nutrition Guide, by Annabel Karmel (DK Publishing, Inc., 2004)

The Girlfriends' Guide to Toddlers: A Survival Manual to the Terrible Two's (and Ones and Threes) From the First Step, the First Potty and the First Word (No) to the Last Blankie, by Vicki Iovine (Penguin Group [USA], 1999)

Dr. Spock's Baby and Child Care, by Benjamin Spock (Simon & Schuster Adult Publishing Group, June 2004)

The Irreducible Needs of Children: What Every Child Must Have to Grow, Learn, and Flourish, by T. Berry Brazelton (Perseus Publishing, 2000)

American Medical Association Complete Guide to Your Children's Health, by D. Kotulak (Random House, 1999)

To Listen to a Child: Understanding the Normal Problems of Growing Up, by T. Berry Brazelton (Addison-Wesley, 1992)

How to Talk So Kids Will Listen & Listen So Kids Will Talk, by Adele Faber (HarperCollins, 2004)

The Optimistic Child: Proven Program to Safeguard Children from Depression & Build Lifelong Resistance, by Martin Seligman (HarperCollins, 1996)

Books, Music, and Activities for One-Year-Olds

Your child needs intellectual stimulation as well as exposure to all sorts of creative expression, including art, dance, and music. All of the books, CDs, and activities in this section are perfect for one-year-olds. Remember, though, that a one-year-old's attention span is typically very short, so even if you're enjoying what you're reading or showing him, he may only pay attention to it for a few minutes. But you can rest assured that the exposure to all of these new things will help his intellectual and emotional development.

Books

Pop-up books are a favorite of young children. Usually these books don't have a long story, but simply a word or two per page. The following books teach colors, numbers, shapes, and other concepts appropriate for one-year-olds.

Color Surprises: A Pop-Up Book, by Chuck Murphy (Simon & Schuster Children's Publishing, 1997)

One to Ten: Pop-Up Surprises (Simon & Schuster Children's Publishing, 1995)

Planes, by Byron Barton (HarperCollins Children's Books, 1998)

Trains, by Byron Barton (HarperCollins Children's Books, 1998)

Trucks, by Byron Barton (HarperCollins Children's Books, 1998)

Inside Freight Train, by Donald Crews (HarperCollins Children's Books, 2001)

Counting Kisses: A Kiss & Read Book by Karen Katz (Simon & Schuster Children's Publishing, 2002)

Wiggle Your Toes, by Karen Katz (Simon & Schuster Children's Publishing, 2006)

Big Red Barn, by Margaret Wise Brown (HarperCollins, 1989)

My Love For You, by Susan L. Roth (Dial Books, 1997)

Barnyard Dance, by Sandra Boynton (Workman Publishing, 1993)

Joy, by Joyce Carol Thomas (Hyperion Books for Children, 2001)

Soothing Goodnight Songs

If you're at a loss, here are some suggestions of songs you can sing to or purchase and download onto your computer. If you can't sing, you can certainly just play them for your baby and listen to them together, but even tone-deaf moms and dads can usually sing in a whisper and sound soothing.

Good Night, My Love
(available on *www.iTunes.com* by Tavares)

Goodnight, my love
Pleasant dreams, sleep tight, my love
May tomorrow be sunny and bright
And draw you closer to me

Before you go
There's just one thing I'd like to know
If your love is still warm for me
Or has it grown cold?

If you should awake in the still of the night
Please have no fear
For I'll be there, you know I care
Please give your love to me, dear, only

Goodnight, my love
Pleasant dreams, sleep tight, my love
May tomorrow be sunny and bright
And draw you closer to me

If you should awake in the still of the night
Please have no fear
For I'll be there, you know I care
Please give your love to me, dear, only

Goodnight, goodnight, my love
Pleasant dreams, sleep tight, my love
May tomorrow be sunny and bright
And draw you closer to me

You Are My Sunshine

(available on *www.iTunes.com* by Norman Blake)

You are my sunshine, my only sunshine.
You make me happy when skies are gray.
You'll never know dear, how much I love you.
Please don't take my sunshine away.

The other night dear, as I lay sleeping,
I dreamt I held you in my arms.

When I awoke dear, I was mistaken,
So I hung my head down and cried.

You are my sunshine, my only sunshine.
You make me happy when skies are gray.
You'll never know dear, how much I love you.
Please don't take my sunshine away.

Dream a Little Dream of Me

(available on *www.iTunes.com* by The Mamas and The Papas)

Stars shining bright above you
Night breezes seem to whisper "I love you"
Birds singin' in the sycamore tree
Dream a little dream of me

Say nighty-night and kiss me
Just hold me tight and tell me you'll miss me
While I'm alone and blue as can be
Dream a little dream of me

Stars fading but I linger on dear
Still craving your kiss
I'm longing to linger till dawn dear
Just saying this

Sweet dreams till sunbeams find you
Sweet dreams that leave all worries behind you
But in your dreams whatever they be
Dream a little dream of me

A Dream Is a Wish Your Heart Makes

(available on *www.iTunes.com* by Julie Andrews)

A dream is a wish your heart makes
When you're fast asleep.
In dreams you will lose your heartache,
Whatever you wish for you keep.

Have faith in your dreams and someday, someday,
Your rainbow will come smiling through.
No matter how your heart is grieving,
If you keep on believing
The dream that you wish will come true.

Oh, no matter how your heart is grieving,
If you keep on believing
The dream that you wish will come true.

When You Wish Upon a Star

(available on *www.iTunes.com* by Rosemary Clooney)

When you wish upon a star
Makes no difference who you are
Anything your heart desires
Will come to you

If your heart is in your dreams
No request is too extreme
When you wish upon a star
As dreamers do

Fate is kind
She brings to those who love
The sweet fulfillment of
Their secret longing

Like a bolt out of the blue
Fate steps in and sees you through
When you wish upon a star
Your dreams come true

Blue Shadows on the Trail

(available on *www.iTunes.com* by Roy Rogers)

Shades of night are falling
As the wind begins to sigh
And the world's silhouetted against the sky.

Blue shadows on the trail
Blue moon shinin' through the trees.
And a plaintive wail from the distance
Comes a driftin' on the evening breeze.

Move along, blue shadows, move along
Soon the dawn will come and you'll be on your way

Until the darkness sheds its veil
There'll be blue shadows on the trail.

Move along, blue shadows, move along
Soon the dawn will come and you'll be on your way

Until the darkness sheds its veil
There'll be blue shadows on the trail.
Shadows on the trail.

Activities

Below are a few ideas for activities that you can do with your one-year-old.

Make a Doll Bed

Take a shoebox and scarf out of your closet and get a pillowcase or piece of fabric. Ask your child to pick out a small doll or stuffed animal. Now, make a big deal out of picking out a special place for your child to put her baby to sleep. Let her wash her baby if she wants and make the bed the way she wants to. Encourage her to feed and sing to the baby. Your toddler may want to do this over and over, changing songs and what she does until she is certain she has created a perfect routine for her baby.

Be an Animal

Get down on all fours and ask your child to do the same. Now, have her imitate you as you pretend to be different animals. As you do this throughout this year, she will be able to name the animals you pretend to be (dog, cat, bear, lion, tiger, pig, sheep, and even a two-legged duck). You can move throughout the house, having her follow you and behaving like different animals. Eventually you'll be able to turn this into a guessing game, as she's able to name the animals. Then, she'll want you to guess which one she is.

Balance on a Ball

Toddlers love exercise balls. They can roll them around. You can also hold your child on its top (she should be sitting) and gently roll the ball, keeping her steady. You can also put her on her belly and do the same thing. You can play games with the ball, too. Roll it back and forth between you, or have her chase it around the room.

Cookie Sheet Magnets

Take a cookie sheet and some magnets and let your child play with the magnets on the cookie sheet. Make sure the magnets aren't too strong (refrigerator magnets are good) because she may have trouble moving them on her own when she's this young.

Treasure Hunt

Go for a walk with your toddler and bring a small shopping bag along with you. Let her collect things, such as pebbles and sticks, to bring home. If you want, you can glue what she brings home to paper, or just leave them in her bag to sort through another day.

Appendix C

Family Budget

A budget comprises three categories: how much income you have, how much money you need, and how much money you have saved. Understanding the details of each of these categories and staying on top of them allows you to not only feel in control of your financial situation, it puts you in control of the situation. Having a complete financial plan will help you afford the things your baby needs as she grows and will help you and your partner plan for your future as a family.

You can use this budget to keep track of a week's spending or a month's (photocopy it to use it as much as you want). You simply need to fill in the appropriate numbers in each space and then add up the columns. You'll be able to see if you have enough money and, if you don't, where you are spending too much. Don't fill in the numbers you *want* to spend each month (or week). Keep close track of your income and spending for a week or two and make educated estimates.

Family Budget Worksheet

INCOME SOURCES

Employment		
Alimony		
Investment income		
Social security		

Other sources of income

_____		
_____		
_____		
_____		
TOTAL INCOME		

SAVINGS

401(k) contributions		
IRA contributions		
Investments		
Bank savings		
TOTAL SAVINGS		

EXPENSES

Housing

Rent/mortgage

Insurance

Maintenance

Food

Groceries

Eating out

School and work lunches

Child care

Tuition

Fees

Transportation

Loan payments

Insurance

Gas

Parking

Public transportation

Healthcare

Medical insurance

Dental insurance

Steady prescriptions

Gym membership

Family recreation

Entertainment

Sports fees

Yearly family vacation

continued

Debt payments

Credit card payments

Student loan payments

Home equity line payments

Loan payments

Personal loan payments

Other expenses

_____

_____

_____

_____

_____

_____

_____

_____

_____

_____

_____

_____

_____

_____

TOTAL EXPENSES

According to the Economic Policy Institute (*www.epinet.org*) the range of basic annual family budgets for a two-parent, two-child family is $31,080 (rural Nebraska) to $64,656 (Boston, Massachusetts). These amounts do not include vacations, education, or other expenses that go beyond basic clothing, housing, and food.

Index